B. Greenriel

The material in this book has been compiled from newspapers and archive material from the following publications: the Birmingham Evening Mail and its Solihull edition; the Warwick County News, the Solihull News; The Birmingham Post; the Solihull Times; the Birmingham Evening Despatch, the Birmingham Gazette, the Knowle Journal, Solihull's St Alphege parish magazine and the Warwick & Warwickshire Advertiser & Leamington Gazette.

Following the demise of the Knowle Journal in 1901, Solihull was not properly served by a weekly newspaper until the arrival of the Warwick County News in 1930.

This publication, which also extensively covered Sutton Coldfield, changed into the Solihull & Warwick County News with the postwar increase in size and importance of the town, and became the Solihull News in 1954, when Solihull became a borough.

Where original text from these publications has been lifted, it has been highlighted in *italics*.

Figures for sterling (pounds; shillings and pence) have been retained wherever appropriate in stories prior to decimalisation in 1971. For younger readers, 12 old pence (1d) equalled one shilling (1s) or 5p: twenty shillings equalled £1 and a guinea was 21s. or *£1.05*.

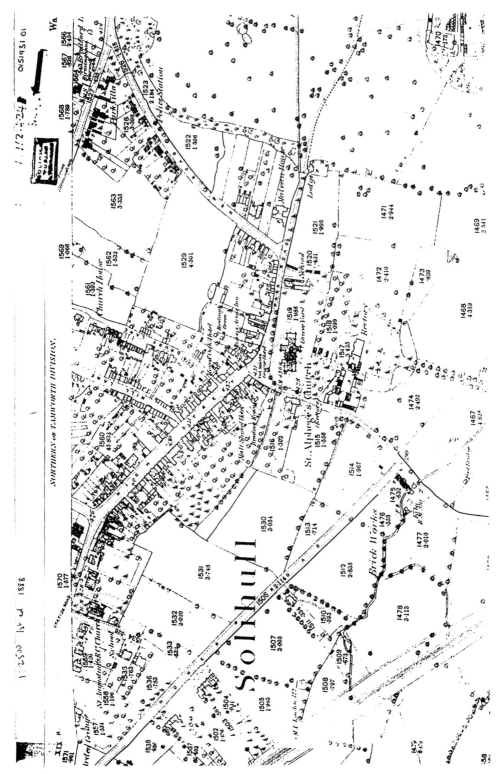

A 25 inches to the mile map of Solihull town centre as it was in 1904.

A Solihull Century

by Robin Jones

BREWIN BOOKS

First published 1997 by
Brewin Books,
Doric House,
56 Alcester Road,
Studley,
Warwickshire, B80 7LG

© Copyright Robin Jones, 1997

ISBN 1 85858 098 6

British Library Cataloguing in Publication Data
A Catalogue record for this book is available from the British Library

Typeset in TimesNewRoman by Avon Dataset Ltd, Bidford on Avon, Warks, B50 4JH
Printed by Alden Press, Osney Mead, Oxford.

to Mom and Dad

ACKNOWLEDGEMENTS

Grateful thanks are due to Sue Bates and the staff at Solihull Central Library's reference section.

Also Solihull Metropolitan Borough Council's technical services department; Midland Independent Newspapers and its subsidiaries, the Birmingham Post & Mail; the Solihull Times and the Solihull News; the Knowle Society; Shirley WI; the family of the late Wynne Thomas; Derek Harrison; George Hill, Alan Williams and Solihull Twinning Association.

Chapter One

EARLY YEARS
1900–13

Solihull will one day be to Birmingham what Kilburn and Chelsea are to London, There are signs and tokens of the impending metamorphosis in the air. Our rusticity is doomed. Some of us who have learned to love the quaint old buildings and ancient streets, with their many historic associations, look to the future with fear and trembling.
(Solihull Monthly Magazine, 1892)

Victorian Birmingham was the workshop of the world and the city of 1,001 trades. Not only had its influence, merchandise and technological innovations spread across the globe, but its expanding urban area was eager to swallow up its green fringes to find space for more factories and workers' homes.

The ancient and then very rural parishes of Yardley and Kings Norton were its first targets and were absorbed into the city early in the next century. Beyond them lay Solihull, known to locals at "the village", a country market town that appeared well out of reach of the big city's despoiling grasp.

The 20th century would be marked by a perennial conflict between the pair, as Solihull, often with its finger in the dyke preventing a tidal wave of development across its prized countryside, proved time and time again that it would not concede ground to its greedy "big brother" to the north as easily as others had done.

And in doing so, it grew from a potential dormitory suburb of Birmingham to a sprawling independent borough where a unique blend of the enriched rural and quality urban earned it a reputation as the "jewel" in the crown of the West Midlands, giving Solihull, for better or worse, a distinctive character of its own.

"Benn Daw", the author of the above magazine extract, continued: *"The ties which link us with the past will not be severed without a struggle; but against what fearful odds will the battle have to be fought!*

"All the energy and brains, the inventive genius of modern civilisation, is arrayed against old age. There can only be one ending to this: Solihull will be modernised.

"The Solihull of today will be swept away by the destroying angel: vandalism and a new and totally different Solihull will spring up in its place."

How true those words would prove.

Salad days

Surrounding by vast tracts of countryside with centuries-old farms in every direction, old Solihull was a collection of semi-rustic cottages interspersed with a plethora of small family-run shops and businesses gathered around four roads – High Street, Warwick Road, Mill Lane and Dog or Drury Lane in the shadow of St Alphege parish church.

It was so incredibly different from the town centre to which we are accustomed today.

Edgar Shepherd, headmaster of Sharmans Cross School in the 1950s, recalled that the High Street of 1909 was a very quiet place – where you might find a pig asleep in the middle of the road or hens running about.

"Shirley and Knowle were places outside our ken", he said, – and a trip to Birmingham was a rare event in one's life."

In the still-cobbled High Street at the corner with Dog Lane stood the premises of Barber Hopkins, who would cut one side of a man's hair and then tell him to turn his chair round so he could cut the other. He would often give musical performances at local dances, he playing the violin and his daughter the harp.

The Hawkes' sweet shop attracted many youngsters, in particular gangs of small boys. They delighted in annoying Mr Hawkes, who also repaired furniture, and if he managed to catch them after morning school, he would drop them in his sawpit so they could not go home for dinner.

Two Miss Pearmans ran the High Street post office. It was said that one was a quite and inoffensive old soul while the other was a crotchety old biddy, and children would hang around to they made sure the right one was duty before they would go in to spend their halfpennies and farthings.

By contrast, a toy and stationery shop was run by the Deebank sisters, who, it was said, would spare no effort to serve even the humblest customer.

Mr Ledbrook had an off licence and operated horse-drawn cabs and a hearse from the Great Western Mews.

At the junction of High Street and Drury Lane stood the Royal Oak, an 18th-century hotel, on the site now occupied by Thomas Cook travel agents. The Gardeners Arms was run by William Lines, who also had Solihull's last independent brewery.

The George Hotel was famous for its bowling green while adjoining the Mason's Arms was a tripe shop – this particular product being as popular then as many people in Solihull might find it horrendous today, and customers brought jugs to carry it away.

The present-day site of Woolworth's in Mill Lane was occupied by a large wisteria-covered house, The Gables, in which lived Dr Adolphus Bernays, and next door was Galloway the tailor, while between Dog Lane and George Road lay allotments. Touchwood Hall, a mansion in dog Lane, was home to the Martineau family.

Along Warwick Road could be found Arthur Hobbins, clock repairer and jeweller, who also ran a house-to-house service on his bicycle. A few doors away traded Harry Roberts the tailor, a deformed man who went around on a hand-driven tricycle. Youngsters would often wait outside his shop to catch the fruit that fell from a fig tree – a rare thing that caused no end of wonder in those days.

A major landmark was Silhill House, formerly the Swan Inn, which stood at the corner of Station Road and Poplar Road with a large assortment of farm buildings. It was the home of the Chattock family for several generations and later the Alldays who held occasional fetes there, unveiling the beautiful gardens hidden behind a long high wall to all.

The property was reputedly haunted and had stood empty for years before it was demolished in 1925.

Opposite lay Harborne House occupied by builders the Thompson brothers and a cottage home to Mrs Johnson – the best chimneysweep in the district.

Another large house in Station Road was Southend, which belonged to the Homer family whose name is preserved by a town centre road name. Next door was Braggs the butchers with its immaculately-kept home delivery team of ponies.

The only bank in the town was Lloyds – in Poplar Road – somewhat ironic as six decades later the whole of this street would become Solihull's "financial quarter".

At the corner of Warwick Road and New Road lay the Spinney which became a carpet of bluebells in spring and the haunt of children during summer holidays. In the other direction going towards Birmingham stood Seven Stars Cottages which had once been an inn. Also giving their name to a modern road, they, like so much of the town centre of 100 years ago, have long since vanished.

Pleasure seeking

The centre of social life in "the village" was the Victorian Public Hall next to the bank in Poplar Road, where a variety of entertainments were held.

The town also had two soccer clubs and a cricket team, along with a musical society, an orchestra and evening classes in commercial subjects.

Copt Heath golf club in Warwick Road opened in 1910 to complement others founded in the district in Victorian times. A science and art exhibition was even started so that locals would put their holidays to practical use.

An annual agricultural show took place in Malvern Park, and local children used to come with buckets and collect as much milk as they liked free of charge from the cows on display. The real big event of them all was the annual flower show, in which anyone and everyone participated.

At Elliots Hall estate alongside the River Blythe at Monkspath, a racecourse drew crowds, with angry headmasters complaining that their pupils went absent on race days.

A short-lived attempt was made to set up a grandiose pleasure gardens for Birmingham daytrippers at the nearby 130-acre Mount Cottage Farm in Cheswick Green, around the medieval moated manor house site called the Mount, with facilities for dancing, tennis, bowls, airgun shooting, swings, donkey rides and sacred concerts on Sundays.

Drawn by attractions like these, many city folk spent their days off visiting rural Solihull, and pubs and roadside tearooms prospered.

State of the art

At a special sitting of the Solihull Petty Sessions, four Birmingham youths of the "peaky" class were charged with stealing a handkerchief, a bottle and a quantity of bread and bacon value one shilling . . . the property of Mr William Green, cowman of Bedlam in the employ of Mr R Ramsden of Chadwick Manor . . . from an engine house on the estate.

The prisoners' names were R Hall, Alfred Francis, Charles Halford and Ernest McCullock, whose ages range from 15 to 17 years.

The first witness was William Greenway, who said . . . he put his dinner at half past eight in the morning in the engine house. At a quarter past twelve he saw the four defendants in the Warwick Road, going in the direction of

Arbour Tree Farm. He identified the handkerchief and bottle produced as his property . . .

PC Clark stated that he received information from the prosecutor that his dinner (which included the articles of the present charge) had been stolen. He went down the road and saw the four prisoners near a rabbit burrow in the Chadwick Manor Park.

He chased them across the park and one of the prisoners dropped the handkerchief, which contained a live rabbit. He chased the prisoners to Temple Balsall Lane where he lost them.

He then went home and got his bicycle and proceeding in the direction of Knowle met the prisoner Hall at Heronfield, and arrested him at two o'clock.

He afterwards went to Solihull and in company with PC Lakin arrested the other three prisoners who were riding in a steamer on the canal.

Hall pleaded not guilty to going into the barn and stealing the dinner, the other prisoners pleaded guilty, and Halford urging the excuse that he had had nothing to eat since the previous day. The prisoners . . . said that they had been to Warwick to enlist, but were unsuccessful.

Halford, previously convicted or an assault, was fined ten shillings with three weeks imprisonment with hard labour in default. The other defendants were fined five shillings and costs or three weeks hard labour. Francis' aunt paid his fine but the others were remanded in custody.

The bench complimented PC Clark for the smartness he showed in following the prisoners, and arrested them.

It showed how absolutely necessary it was that police officers should be provided with bicycles.

(Knowle Journal, 1900)

The grass is always greener . . .

Birmingham industrialists who chose to escape the smog and grime that their factories generated used their new-found wealth to uproot their families to the more pleasant pastures to the south, a move facilitated in mid-Victorian times by the opening of the London to Snow Hill railway on which they could commute.

The middle-class exodus which created the settlement of Dorridge also saw large red-brick houses complete with servants' quarters mushroom along Warwick Road, Blossomfield Road, Church Hill Road and other main routes near the town's railway station. Solihull's population doubled between 1891 and 1911 to more than 10,000.

Alfred Bird, Birmingham's "Custard King", who laid the foundation stone of Shirley Institute on 12 March 1903, moved into Tudor Grange and a member of the Pears soap family acquired Chadwick Manor.

At first, builders picked plots between existing properties in Solihull town centre for "infilling" but soon, demand outstripped supply, and houses became the final crop for the surrounding fields.

Ashleigh Road arrived in 1904 and was followed by Alderbrook Road, The Crescent and Broad Oaks Road by 1913.

Administration

Solihull had become a rural district council in 1894, encompassing the parishes of Baddesley Clinton, Barston, Bushwood, Elmdon, Knowle, Lapworth, Nuthurst, Packwood, Tanworth and Temple Balsall.

It was to be the first of many boundary changes for Solihull over the next 100 years – in fact the town has experienced more territorial shifts than even Poland in the 20th century.

The new council which had wider powers than its predecessor, the Solihull Rural Sanitary Authority, and its office in two semi-detached villas in Streetsbrook Road was established in 1905.

First concern

The curtain was raised on the 20th century with the whole country locked in armed conflict in South Africa – the second Boer War.

Several Solihull men enlisted and their letters back home vividly describing battle conditions were often published in the parish magazine. One, Trooper Harry Cheadle, of the South Staffordshire Company of Imperial Yeomanry, told of the capture of Slobberts Nek, the surrender of 6,000 enemy troops – and of a friendly fire incident – no censorship here whatsoever:

They (the Boers) commence shelling us very soon, and General Paget, who was supposed to be assisting us on the left, opened fire on us with a 15-pounder.

He burst three shrapnel shells too close to us to be pleasant before he discovered his mistake.

A party-like atmosphere was evident in Solihull's High Street and also throughout the locality during celebrations to mark the relief of Mafeking in 1900.

The passing of the greatest age?

Despite the all-pervading sense of timelessness among the inhabitants of old "Silhill", the new century heralded major changes to society both national and local, and set new challenges accordingly.

> *Since last January God has taken from us several of the chiefest of our people, and one and all have been sorrowing that the old familiar faces are seen no more. As one by one we lose the links which connect the village life with the modern community and township into which we are rapidly growing, the reality of the change passing over us becomes more and more apparent, and will, now that we have entered upon another century, appeal to us, perhaps, with even deeper intensity.*
>
> *Of one thing we can all be assured – that our responsibilities become greater as the world grows older . . .*
>
> (Rev Thomas Beedle Beedle Harvey Brooks, Rector of Solihull, January 1901)

The longest and perhaps the greatest of all eras in British history came to an end in 1901 with the death of Queen Victoria.

Flying the flag and proud of it. Knowle schoolboys dressed up for a special party held to celebrate the relief of Mafeking during the Boer War, the major international news item in 1900.

The Square in Solihull town centre decorated for the coronation of Edward VII in 1902, delayed because of fears about the ageing heir's health.

Solihull's Dr Adolphus Bernays, a prominent local figure early this century, and his chauffeur Joseph Fripp, in the grounds of his brother's house in Stanmore, Middlesex. Dr Bernays car, AC995, was registered in 1907.

Now the A41 Warwick Road, this is sylvan Copt Heath Avenue, Knowle Road in the early years of the century – and not a car in sight. Was this the route that the intrepid PC Clark took to Solihull on his bicycle when he apprehended the dastardly villains who had stolen a workman's bacon sandwich? (Chapter One)

Ah! Who of us anticipated, as we entered hopefully on another century, that its opening month was to be darkened by a grief so deep – that the end of the long reign matchless in the history of nations was so close at hand (Rev Harvey Brooks) Churches throughout Solihull were packed with mourners and the pulpit and choir stalls were draped with black cloth.

Her son Edward VII was by then well into his years and the original date for his coronation was postponed through his ill health. In Solihull as elsewhere festivities to mark the occasion were placed on hold accordingly.

The eventual Westminster Abbey service was mirrored by one in St Alphege church to the minute, followed by a procession to Malvern Park – then still in private hands – where a sports day and a children's tea was held before the celebrations ended with fireworks.

The park was also the venue for similar festivities to mark the accession of King George V and Queen Mary in 1910, when a procession led by four local Boer War veterans on horseback paraded through High Street, Poplar Road, Warwick Road and New Road, beneath triumphal arches erected along with Venetian masts and bunting. Commemorative mugs were given to 600 children while girls from the elementary school performed maypole dances.

A figure forever linked with a less savoury image of Victorian Britain, thanks to Charles Dickens, was the parish beadle.

For thirty years James Holliday carried out the role in Solihull together with that of sexton and also what remained of the old parish clerk's duties until his sudden death in 1902 on his way to evening service. He was buried in his uniform.

Also immortalised in *Oliver Twist* was the poor law institution or workhouse, which paupers would have to enter in order to receive relief.

Life inside was designed to be moderately unpleasant, making the able-bodied inmates wish to leave as soon as possible and live by their own labours. Solihull's workhouse in Union Road was very active in 1900, when it held 118 inmates, with 107 tramps passing through the district in a fortnight.

Frequent attempts were, however, made by local well-wishers to relieve the monotony of life there – which as a result was probably nowhere as bad as portrayed in the novel. Mrs Wright of Hillfield Hall entertained the old people to tea and those who could not go received presents. The rector appealed for local entertainers to perform there while other townsfolk donated produce.

The demise of the old order was locally apparent in the death of magnate Joseph Gillott in 1903.

He was the son of the pioneering Birmingham penmaker of the same name and used his inherited wealth to buy up vast land holdings around Catherine-de-Barnes, including Ravenshaw, Field and Cow Hayes farms and Berry Hall.

Following the trend of the benevolent Victorian landowner, Joseph Gillott junior founded a school at Catney and was instrumental in bringing a decent doctor to Solihull. He was, said Rev Harvey Brooks, "rightly beloved by all that knew him".

His massive country gentleman's estate was sold off by Birmingham auctioneer Edward Betteridge in parcels. There would never be another like it in Solihull again.

Equality for all

A town inhabited on one hand by paupers and tramps and on the other extreme by a man who owned half the countryside to the east might well be hailed as a the perfect showcase for the class system of the day. Not so, the Knowle Journal of 1901 reliably informs us:

There are many who express the opinion that there is one law for the rich and another for the poor; but this view cannot morally be entertained in Knowle or Solihull, at least with regard to the dog muzzling order.

It matters not whether the cur belongs to a person of high degree or a non entity – it is all the same if the canine friend is found by the police devoid of muzzle or a collar with the owner's name inscribed thereon.

And thus we have it – one week a shopkeeper or mechanic summoned for the offence – and the next week a doctor's wife and solicitor.

Country bliss

Nobody better than Olton resident Edith Holden, whose home, Gowan House in Kineton Green Road, is thankfully still there today, captured the essence of the rural Solihull of the day, but we had to wait nearly three-quarters of a century to enjoy the fruits of her 1906 notebook, *The Country Diary of An Edwardian Lady*.

She described the lanes on a walk through Catherine-de-Barnes, Hampton-in-Arden, Elmdon and Bickenhill were "fragrant with wild roses, and honeysuckle, and the breeze came to us over the hedges laden with the perfume of the clover fields and grass meadows".

Edith died in 1920, drowning in the Thames at Kew as she attempted to gather chestnut buds.

Unwillingly to school?

Solihull's centuries-old grammar school was already among the undisputed flagships of the Midland educational system by the turn of the century.

Most local children, however, came from families whose resources did not stretch to school fees and therefore attended either the Park Road girls and infants school or the Mill Lane boys school. The Park Road school and Bentley Heath School, which had an extension in 1902 opened by the Bishop of Coventry, were run by the United Charities while the Mill Lane school was the responsibility of trustees.

Former pupils at Park Road later recalled how they used to huddle around the stove in the middle of the senior school's large classroom in winter – but copped for it when the wind changed direction and blew the smoke back in their faces.

When a funeral was held at the adjoining parish church, the windows had to be kept shut and the pupils remained quiet, but when a wedding was in progress, they would be allowed to line up outside and watch.

Land in adjoining the school in Mill Lane was set aside for gardening, two boys working together on one allotment. The gardens were described as being "particularly well cared for" and prizes were awarded.

A year-round education could not always be guaranteed:

It was most unfortunate that it was necessary to close the schools for the last

three weeks of the term, for it means practically no education for two months!
 However, it was. not possible to curtail the usual holidays as the teachers had made their arrangements to spend the time with relations and friends.
 Let us hope that the children are making themselves particularly useful in their homes, and that when they are about in fields and lanes, they will keep their eyes and ears open and thus learn the number of lessons which are taught by earth's many voices.

(Parish magazine)

Despite teachers' unorthodox holiday arrangements, standards at the elementary schools were regularly praised by inspectors.

In these early years, however, we saw the beginnings of a debate that would in much later decades shake the structure of Solihull's education system by its foundations:

It is difficult to make the little people in an infants school understand that some are better than others at their lessons (sometimes grown-up folks can't understand it, and so they do not "esteem others better than themselves") so we got over the difficulty by giving an illustrated book to every child.
 The distribution took place at the school by Mrs Harvey Brooks, to the very great pleasure of the children, who beamed with delight.

(Rev Harvey Brooks)

On the other side of the town lay St Augustine's Roman Catholic school in Herbert Road, founded in the previous century by Canon O'Sullivan.

Ironically, his school drew larger numbers of Protestant children because their parents were impressed by its academic standards.

His niece Mary O'Gorman was headmistress in the early years of this century and was considered a veritable battleaxe by pupils.

They would chant: *"Miss O'Gorman is a good girl, she goes to church on Sundays, and prays to God to give her strength to wallop the kids on Mondays."*

In addition to endless recitations of times tables and long prayers, she taught the boys when to raise their caps and how to walk a lady along the street – illustrating the idea with a chalk line as the pavement edge.

A former pupil recalled:"She would knock the pen through my book to make me write with my right hand because I was left handed."

A much smaller educational establishment was Powell's school which stood at the top of Church Hill Road opposite the rectory and was run by a Miss Cartland, who was related to the pink-attired romantic novelist Dame Barbara Cartland.

Villages like Shirley, Hockley Heath and Hampton-in-Arden had their own schools.

In 1903, a small party of nuns who had fled from religious persecution in France arrived in St Bernards Road, Olton, and founded a select school for young ladies in Olton Court, a large house.

The convent school opened that September with four boarders who studied needlework, French and art. It grew in strength and eventually won official recognition as a fully-fledged secondary school.

Scouting

The Scouts are 'the eyes of the army' and so a scout is trained to be alert. keen and athletic but a good scout is one who has also learned to be chivalrous, self-controlled and God-fearing.

(Rev Harvey Brooks)

The St Alphege clergy set up the town's first scout group after the movement was launched by General Robert Baden Powell, hero of Mafeking, after the Boer War. Solihull's first girl guide was Doris Willcox, who later became a doctor and married the popular local surgeon Paul Quinet. She and her sister gathered together a group of friends to start a group in their home town.

Their 1st Solihull company was registered with eight members in 1915 and later inspected by Baden Powell in Birmingham's Cannon Hill Park.

The smallest church

The booming Solihull population increased the workload of the rector and his team, who served not only St Alphege but mission churches at Catherine-de-Barnes and Bentley Heath, not forgetting the workhouse.

In 1908 royal approval was given for Olton to be split off to form a new "consolidated chapelry" with St Margarets church at its centre.

The tiny farming hamlet of Shelley Green, now engulfed by the Monkspath and Hillfields estates, was targeted by a clergy determined to bring the Word to everyone in the parish.

In 1908, a harvest festival service was held in a cottage in nearby Widney Lane, and for some years a Sunday school attended by 30 children had thrived there. With donations of help from many quarters, a new mission church was erected in a field at Hillfield Farm, and became the smallest in the district.

Olton was given a congregational church in Kineton Green Road in 1901, while Shirley, which boasted a Baptist tradition dating back to 1797, had a new chapel built in Stratford Road 1911.

The Rev R J Braithwaite provided it in memory of his wife's parents, the Guys of Wednesbury, hence the name Guy Memorial Chapel. A school followed in 1913.

A Wesleyan chapel erected in Stratford Road, Shirley in 1903 burned down 24 years later. It was the predecessor of Shirley Methodist church.

Shirley's darkest days

In 1900, an inquiry was held at the workhouse into a bid by Solihull District Council for power to light the parish with gas lamps.

For the council, Mr Thompson said that Shirley and Olton residents had become concerned about frequent road accidents. At that time only Solihull ward with its 3,400 population was lit.

Mr Hemus, speaking for Shirley, said that people came out to live there only in summertime, but left in the winter, saying that "they could not stay in dark Shirley". But Solihull's farmers voiced their strong opposition . . . saying that they did not want their cowsheds illuminated under any circumstances.

An emergency service

The Solihull Volunteer Fire Brigade took nothing from the public purse and relied entirely on donations and the goodwill of its staff to give their time freely.

A horse-drawn engine was kept in a station behind the Barley Mow pub. At first the horses had to be caught in the meadow before an emergency could be attended.

On 21 July 1911, the brigade attended a blaze which gutted Bentley Manor, the home of North Country squire Wickham Martin. The alarm was raised by a passer-by who saw flames leaping from a bedroom window and told a cyclist – who rode three miles to the Solihull station.

Captain Thompson and his valiant crew attended the scene "as speedily as possible" but found the house "a huge cauldron of fire". The only water supply was a pond – and soon the firemen's hose became choked with mud.

So they gave up on the manor and instead saved the outbuildings – still earning the praise of the large crowd that gathered.

Beware the plague!

> *It has been thought wise, in view of the fact that there have been a few cases of fever in the village, to postpone the visit of the London children, who were to have arrived on July 25th, until a later date, trusting that then there will be less reason for apprehension.*
>
> *If in a month's time they are able to come, we hope that the kindness of several of our friends may be repeated this year, in asking the children to tea, as in former years, and so add to the happiness which these city bairns feel so keenly, but which to them comes so seldom.*
>
> (Parish magazine, July 1902)

Fears were also expressed that these London children might bring smallpox following an outbreak in several parts of the capital in 1902. Measles also closed the infants' school for part of the summer term in 1913.

At the time Solihull had no hospital and medical knowledge was, of course, light years behind modern times.

In 1910, an isolation hospital was built in Henwood Lane near Catherine-de-Barnes for patients with smallpox and other notifiable diseases in a joint exercise between Solihull and its sister rural district council of Meriden.

Kings of the road

A car may have been a rare novelty at the turn of the century – but road traffic convictions were certainly not.

At Solihull Police Court, Haulier James Cox of Lode Lane was fined five shillings for driving a horse and trap without lights in Poplar Road. Another haulier, Joseph Rabin, of Kingswood, was fined 2s 6d for leaving a horse and cart unattended in Station Road, Knowle.

Neither did the dubiously-named offence of "joyriding" or the police chases connected with it begin with the petrol engine.

Bentley Manor, the home of Squire Wykeham-Martin, after the blaze which beat Solihull's volunteer firemen in 1911. It was built in 1857 as a hunting lodge by the family who were Lords of the Manor of Packwood. In recent years it has been converted into a nursing home.

Women haymaking in what was once Solihull's rural fringe at St Bernard's Grange in Olton in 1913. These fields were built over after the Second World War.

In 1900, Solihull's RDC's Inspector of Nuisances, William Harris, left his horse and trap outside the Horse Shoes pub in Coventry Road, Sheldon. Emerging after a few minutes, he found that the trap had gone.

Enlisting the help of PC Hunt, he obtained another trap and pursued two boys who had taken his own in a bid to ride to Coventry, catching up with them at Bickenhill. The elder of the two, John Miles, aged 17, was sent to a reform school until he was 19.

The age where the car was undisputed king was still many years off, but one entrepreneur had the foresight to predict its arrival.

In 1909, William Bennett Archer realised how busy the junction of Stratford Road and Marshall Lake Road in Shirley would become, and bought a prime site on the corner.

A petrol station was built there in 1928, and further extensions saw the addition of a repair shop and then a showroom, selling Standard cars. In modern times Archers became a major Rover dealership and the site is now the giant Evans Halshaw showroom.

Don't fence me in!

Building speculators were also eagerly surveying Shirley's fields for housing development.

In 1900, the Great Western Railway had its eagle eyes on the land necessary for building the North Warwickshire branch line which opened up Hall Green, Yardley Wood and Shirley to developers.

The Nags Head Hotel in Hockley Heath on 20 June 1914 with a pioneering Midland Red bus 23-seater which ran a service from Birmingham to Stratford-upon-Avon from then until 1928. The pub, given a major facelift in 1996, was for several years known as the Wayfarer.

"God's Wonderful Railway" infuriated locals by obstructing footpaths around Earlswood Lakes which it claimed as its own, by installing gates and posts in what was described as "land jumping."

In immediate retaliation, the Solihull RDC surveyor with 10 men went to the lakes and tore down the obstructions to let visitors back in again . . . only for the railway's labourers to reinstate them an hour later.

As soon as the fences were back up again, the surveyor pulled them down for the second time. The railwaymen retaliated and re-erected them again, and so the process continued . . .

The *Knowle Journal* reported:"It appeared as if the stupid game of re-erecting the posts as they were demolished would continue indefinitely had not the surveyor . . . wisely withdrew to bring the matter again before the council."

To little avail – the fences disappeared and reappeared at least twice daily as the two sides continued in conflict – until the GWR finally reinforced them with tar and iron bars.

Ironically the GWR had sought to close the paths to stop people using the lakes as a pleasure ground, yet when the branch, the last to be built in the West Midlands was finally opened in 1908, the three canal feeder reservoirs were heavily promoted as an attraction for passengers!

Shirley's railway station indeed attracted commuters, despite being well away from the village centre, and Burman Road was the first of many to be built . . . as the new urban fringe spread to the west.

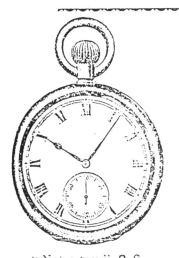

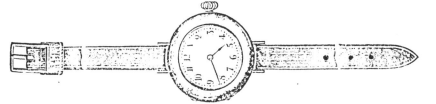

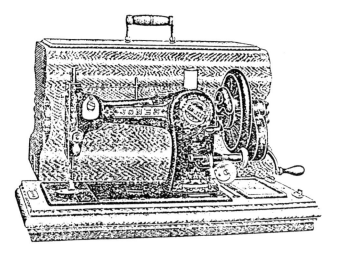

Chapter Two

THE GREAT WAR AND AFTERWARDS
1914–1921

Solihull was at war in 1914.

The *Warwick & Warwickshire Advertiser & Leamington Gazette* had no doubt whatsoever about it.

Everyone rallied to arms to fight the menace from the enemy within:

The farmers . . . have resolved to wage war on wood pigeons which are playing havoc with the clover seeds. Arrangements are being made so that there shall be guns in every covert in the county so that the pests may be got at when they come home to roost. The war of extermination will be waged on Thursday afternoons beginning on February 5 and five consecutive Thursday beginning at 3pm until dusk.

Outside the borders of the rural district, however, far greater tensions than wood pigeons were mounting on several different fronts. A 'triple alliance' of miners, transport workers and railwaymen were threatening an all-out strike in support of the latter's claim for union recognition and a 48-hour week, while Ireland was on the brink of civil war.

Europe was rocked by the assassination of the Hapsburg heir Archduke Franz Ferdinand in Sarajevo, Bosnia, on June 28, plunging the tiny nation states of the Balkans into renewed turmoil and eventually the rest of the continent into an armed conflict, the like of which humanity had never experienced before.

The German invasion of neutral Belgium on August 4 brought Britain into the turmoil, and men everywhere answered the call to patriotic duty by flocking to swell the ranks of the armed forces without the initial need for conscription.

Many thought the war would be over by Christmas, and precious few raised moral questions over their part in the conflict. From his summer holiday retreat in Ballintum, Scotland, Rev Harvey Brooks told his parishioners:

A righteous indignation at the cruel oppression of small and innocent states has compelled us to unsheathe the sword to relieve the oppressed, and we cannot but feel that, even though with great sacrifices, our cause must prevail: for the Judge of all the earth must do right . . .

Everyone *is wanted. To every able-bodied man comes the call to arms; and to everybody else comes the call to service at home . . .*

Don't take notice of any unofficial rumours; we can quite trust the authorities to tell us everything when it is wise that we should know.

By October, 34 Solihull men had enlisted in the army since war was declared.

Mrs Frank Chatterly, of Craycombe, Birmingham Road, became local secretary of the Soldiers and Sailors Association, which set out to tackle cases of want and distress among the families of active servicemen while a special committee was set up to handle other hardship cases arising from the war. Townsfolk were urged not to give private relief without first telling the committee so that it would be fairly distributed.

Another organisation with Mr J W Hall of Kineton, Warwick Road, as secretary, was set up to help an influx of Belgian refugees, collecting furniture, food and books in French from residents.

Home truths

The first names added to the town's roll of honour after being killed in action in the early weeks of conflict were Claude Percival Wilks, aged 22, of the Kings Royal Rifles, a prize-winning gardener and a member of Solihull's football team who regularly attended the church at Catherine-de-Barnes, and John Edward Ratcliffe, aged 23, of the Royal Warwickshire Regiment, whose parents lived in Widney Cottage, Bentley Heath.

It soon became obvious that the war would not be over within months and Solihull's home affairs would take a very poor second place to it for a long time to come.

In December, the rector wrote: "The appalling amount of sorrow far and wide caused by the war must naturally mar our usual Christmas rejoicings . . .

The ravages of war soon began to bite hard at home. For many years the church had held an "American sale" whereby items of clothing were donated for resale to the poor of less fortunate parishes at low cost. Now, the appeal was amended for clothing "for our own poor."

Solihull's clergy also appealed for new bell ringers, the regulars having gone to serve in Flanders: "We must remember that the thought of church bells ringing at home goes far towards cheering the men who have gone from home to fight their country's battles".

Your country still needs YOU

Meanwhile, Lord Kitchener's jingoistic calls to enlisted out unabated. A Cadet Corps under the auspices of the War office was formed to allow boys between 12 and 18 to prepare for service.

Intended as a "feeder" to the Territorial Army, its headquarters were the schools in Park Road and its leader was Lieutenant Riley of Alderbrook Road. Parade was staged every Tuesday at 8pm.

A first Army" – the Volunteer Corps – came into its own, and it Solihull a "goodly number" promised to join, being prevented for various reasons from serving on the front line.

"Even if some of us are too old to do the 'goose step', we can do *something,"* the appeal ran.

By January 1915, 238 Solihull men were serving in the armed forces, with four listed as prisoners of war, the figures rising by the month.

A small fund was set up to send every POW a parcel each fortnight. The girls from the elementary school raised 3s per fortnight to "adopt" Private William Green in this way, while the boys took on Leading Seaman Chubb, and children at Catherine-de-Barnes school made sandbags.

A postcard received in August 1916 from a Solihull soldier taken prisoner in Germany showing the interior of "the church which we have made here".
"It is some consolation to find that among all the horrors of captivity some of our men are provided with places where they may meet together to worship their God and ours," added the parish magazine editor.

The Voluntary Auxiliary Detachment turned Springfield House near Knowle into a hospital for wounded soldiers during the Firs world War. Some of the first servicemen to be nursed there are pictured outside Norton Cottage in March 1915.

Medical relief

Of course, war action was not limited to the military: parish magazine treasure Miss Roper departed for Red Cross service in southern France.

Solihull had its own Red Cross hospital for soldiers, at the Hermitage in Hermitage Road, a property loaned by Mr Lindner which had received 82 patients by the start of 1915, most of them, we were told, suffered from "sickness" and frostbite rather than actual wounds.

The establishment was run for more than four years by Miss Townshend as commandant with the invalids arriving by train to Solihull station.

Several local residents lucky enough to afford motor cars took the convalescing service-men for trips out, or to evenings entertainments such as "lantern lectures" and concerts.

Other large houses were also pressed into service as military hospitals by the Volunteer Aid Detachment – Springfield House between Knowle and Temple Balsall, the Institute in Hampton-in-Arden and the Berkswell rectory.

Solihull may have covered only a very tiny fraction of the map of Britain yet there seemed no end of demand for its services in this field – a fact that brought home the true extent of the hitherto unimaginable horrors taking place on the Western front in name of king and country.

A branch of the North Warwickshire War Hospital Supply Depot was established at Copt Heath golf club and an appeal issued for volunteers to help prepare bandages and swabs. In 1916 it was augmented by a needlework branch at Northmede in Station Road, a property loaned by Hugh Chattock.

A Letter to Solihull's postman

> *Tuesday, April 11th, 1916.*
>
> *Dear Mr & Mrs Harrison,*
>   *Kindly excuse me taking the liberty of writing to you, but I think it is my duty, and only right that you should have knowledge of your son's bravery in the little affair where I was granted the D.C.M.*
>   *As I dare say you are aware, there were six men, including myself, on the team, and all of us were very amicable towards each other. On the morning that the mine was exploded we were "standing to." Consequently we were not caught unawares.*
>   *The vibration caused by the explosion was far above normal, and the mine was one of the largest yet seen out here.*
>   *Before the earth had settled. I gave the order to "stand to follow me," and I might say that your son was the first to do so, and, although he was not numbered off at the time as my second or "right hand man," he acted as such and stood by me all time, greatly assisting me under trying conditions and circumstances.*
>   *He is to be congratulated, and I know you will be proud of him. I wish is that they gave two D.C.M.'s. Anyway, I have got him with me still, and I shall take and help him at all times.*
>   *Yours sincerely, C. MATTOCK.*
>   *Sergeant. Lewis Gun Section*

Women's work

> *The representative of the Board of Agriculture attended meetings in the Board Room of our workhouse, at which he explained the nature of what is required, and the paramount necessity of women working at farms to take the place of men who have been called up.*
>
> *In other countries women have always done a very large share of such work. It is new for us, but the idea is catching on, and in many parts of our country large numbers of women are doing excellent work. It consists of general farm work: vesting, hoeing, fruit picking, etc.*
>
> *We have made quite a good start. Farmers, or private people wanting work done in their gardens, and who are ready to do such work, should apply to Mrs. Harvey Brooks, President of our local committee, or to Mrs. Allport, Homer Road, who is Hon Secretary.*
>
> (Rev Harvey Brooks)

The Women's Land Army was formed in 1917 when Britain was down to three weeks' supply of food.

Women were recruited by the government and paid by farmers, taking on a variety of jobs from milkmaids to tractors drivers, shepherdesses and even thatchers.

A teacher's war

Sergeant E H Schofield, one of the assistant masters at the town boys school, wrote to Solihull from Bristol Hospital in October 1916 where he was recovering from a shrapnel wound in the back:

> *Our Division has seen its share of the Somme fighting since July 1st. We were rushed off at minute's notice up to Delville Wood, High Wood and Longueval, and saw some terrible scrapping for the fortnight we were there. We took a portion of High Wood, and the whole of Delville Wood and Longueval.*
>
> *On September 3rd, after reorganisation, we took part in another advance. Our objective was Falfamont Farm, in front of Combles.*
>
> *We took the place, and it was about 2 p.m. when I got my wound. It is a nice "Blighty" one, not too serious.*
>
> *On the following Sunday I found myself in Beaufort Hospital. Now having a fine time – some fellow in wounded soldier's togs, going out to wounded soldier's outings, &c.*
>
> *Our Battalion got badly cut up before we went 'over the top.' We had lost every officer in our company, and I found myself 2nd in command. However the boys are doing finely, and sweeping everything before them.*
>
> *I don't know how Burgess got on. I saw him just before we went into action, and he was all right then. Remember me to all the boys. When I come out of hospital I get ten day's at home. I will come round and see you.*

Rowland Hill Burgess, another assistant at the school, was in fact killed in action while a third, Mr A Peppitt, also went to the front. The headmaster, Mr E J P Orrett, was called up in March 1917.

The local clergy did not exempt themselves from front line service. The Rev Charles

Wormald was taken at a week's notice to the Dardanelles as forces chaplain, while Mr S P Riley, who had been minister at the Catherine-de-Barnes church, had six days to prepare himself after volunteering. After the war he became vicar at Shirley.

Terror from the skies

Those who stayed at home could not longer escape the carnage inflicted by the enemy, for this terrible conflict introduced the concept of aerial bombardment on a massive scale.

Fears of an invasion from the skies had gripped the Midlands in May 1909 around the time that the Kaiser's men were demonstrating their superiority in the field of airship technology. Residents of Small Heath in Birmingham were astonished to see a cigar-shape object hovering over the British Standard Armaments factory on several occasions, while newspapers reported that Britain had been invaded by a fleet of phantom ships.

No invasion materialised, and the airships were found to belong to the British agents of a continental car manufacturer which had been using them as giant advertising hoardings.

However, Zeppelin airships which crossed Solihull skies during the war proved less benign.

Bombs were dropped behind the Red Lion public house in Stratford Road, Shirley, and at a number of other locations including Box Trees near Hockley Heath . . .

St Patrick's church in Salter Street, Earlswood, is believed to contain the unmarked grave of a German soldier who died while interned at Elliotts Hall, now the Trustee Savings Bank college in Creynolds Lane, Monkspath, and then used as a POW camp.

His name was disguised in the church records – probably because of the anti-Hun feelings of the day.

The shape of things to come?

> *Seventeen Germans living in various parts of the county were arrested this week and taken to Warwick police station and . . . were removed to a concentration camp.*
> Warwick & Warwickshire Advertiser & Leamington Gazette May 1915.

"Germany's allies" in our midst

An enemy far worse than even the wood pigeon was at work in Solihull, the local press reported:

Flies are disease carriers. They have caused more disease in Europe this year than any other owing to the war. There will be more intercommunication between east and west owing to the continued movements to and from of German troops, more traffic between England and the continent owing to the passage of our troops. Flies once more are disease carriers, therefore kill them at any time but more than ever this year.

The moral is still the same. The only good fly is a dead fly and he should be burned at once.

The war shrine

Easter 1917 saw a huge crowd gather in The Square for the dedication of a shrine in memory of 39 men who had fallen during the conflict.

The shrine was given by a parishioner, designed by Mr Elphege Pippet and constructed by Charles Timms of builders Thompsons.

> *These gallant soldiers have died for the emancipation of the human race from the most terrible tyranny that has even threatened the world, and this war shrine will be a reminder to us of their glorious death*
>
> (Rev Harvey Brooks)

All conkering

A Food Control Campaign launched throughout the country in 1917 again highlighted the vast shortages that beset Britain, both for home use and at the front. In September, a fresh appeal was made by the Government – for conkers.

The Director of Munitions reminds us of the great value of the horse chestnut crop, by the use of which in the making of munitions a large quantity of grain which would otherwise be required for the purpose can be released for use as food. Parents are asked to encourage their boys to collect the chestnuts and forego the pleasure which they naturally have in using them as "Conqs."

Arrangements win be made for collecting at the schools, etc., and notice will be duly given. This is a splendid opportunity for children to help towards food supply, and I am sure they will like to feel they are doing their bit in this, as in so many other ways.

Nuts should not be gathered until they are fully ripe. Unripe nuts are of no value for the purpose.

Children must not knock about the trees; this is quite unnecessary, as the nuts drop when they are ripe.

Honoured for gallantry

A former Solihull choirboy, Albert Heywood, was one of five brothers who joined the forces. At 19 he had opted for a life in the ministry and spent five years working in a large parish in Bolton, Lancashire. Afterwards, he entered St Aidan's theological college and gained an "honourable position", while spending his spare time among the poor of the Liverpool slums.

After two years he enlisted, attaining the rank of Second Lieutenant. Six months at the front ended when he fell while leading his men.

Rev A Wye, vicar of St James, Bolton, wrote: "His character was beyond reproach and his sincerity was manifest to all who knew him."

Another local, Corporal J H Frost, was awarded the DCM. The parish magazine reported:

Although severely wounded in the hand, he worked his way under intense fire from shell-hole to shell-hole until about 40 yards ahead of his company. Here he kept up a fire with rifle grenades on the enemy, causing a large number of casualties. When some men were able to reach him after dark, it was found that he had been twice more wounded.

Lance Corporal Edgar Shepherd received the Military Medal for heroics in an action which left him wounded and discharged from the army. An officer who witnesses his heroics in September 1917 wrote: *His battalion were taking part in a rather big attack m the sector, and, during the operations, he and his officer and another man became separated from the remainder of the company.*

Directly facing them was a German strong point, commonly known as a "pill-box." From this position the enemy were doing a considerable amount of damage to our men, and seeing this, the officer dashed forward, closely followed by Edgar and the other lad, and between them they succeeded in capturing the position, together with the whole of the occupants (about 18 Germans) and several guns.

The difficulty then lay in letting the officers of the Battalion know that this position was in our hands and in securing a force to take charge of the prisoners. This was done by Edgar, who safely delivered the message only to be struck in the back with a bullet just as he had completed his plucky work. The wound which he sustained is a dangerous one, and he was most fortunate to escape with his life.

007 in 1917?

While many such acts of bravery in the hell of no man's land received public praise, the feats of other local men went unrecorded, sometimes by necessity.

It was 15 years before the exploits of an British intelligence officer emerged – and then only because he was summonsed before Solihull Police Court for non-payment of household rates.

Even then, the Scottish-born man was not named in court when represented by solicitor A Parton-Smith – because of an alleged kidnap attempt that had been made against him.

The court heard that he was sent to Russia and became a member of the Czar's own flying corps on the eastern front. After the October Revolution, he was appointed to the country's ministry of transport under the provisional government.

Come the Bolshevik takeover – and the spy was thrown into jail, until one morning when he was taken out to be "shot at dawn". That turned out to be a ruse to make him divulge information.

Confinement in a communist jail damaged his health, but he was able to escape and return to Britain.

His ill health, however, prevented him from holding down a job and he also suffered from malaria. And all those years later he was still living in fear – because "the tentacles of the Soviet regime were far reaching".

A triple marriage

Happier stories also emerged from the years of conflict. A couple who were to make Solihull their home met on an Egyptian beach during the war in the Mediterranean.

While serving with the 1st/7th Manchester Regiment in Turkey, Foster was sent to recuperate in Alexandria. While walking on a beach there in 1915, he met his Maltese wife, Eleonora. They dated for four years, during which Percy spent much time on active service in Europe. Because of their different religions, they underwent three marriage ceremonies.

At 10am on their big day, they were married at the British Consulate: at 3pm they attended a ceremony at the Protestant church; and at 5pm they again tied the knot at a Catholic one.

Their reception went on until 7am the next day . . . because martial law was in force and nobody could go home. After some years in Bristol, the couple, who had four children, moved to Harwood Grove in Shirley.

How times have changed!

> We all know how terribly heroic little Serbia has suffered and is still suffering . . . the people of Serbia and Montenegro are not only starving but actually dying of hunger.
>
> The Serbians are people of remarkable intelligence and erudition, and numbers of Serbian boys are now in our public schools and universities. These, too, require our help. With a view to helping us to understand Serbian needs...we have arranged for a meeting in the rectory grounds. Miss Frances Parklnson who has spent some years in Serbia will tell us all about it.
>
> (Rev Harvey Brooks)

Spreading the word

"The village" was still not considered sizeable or important enough to have its own weekly newspaper in these dark days, and the St Alphege parish magazine was crucial as a means of conveying community news.

However, its influence was far wider than even the rector had suspected:

I often hear of parishioners sending copies of our magazine to our boys at the Front, who naturally enjoy reading what goes on in connection with the parish where their homes are. One of the boys home on leave told me that when he was wandering through the streets of Albert, to his surprise and delight he picked up a recent copy of our magazine.

A memo from the headmaster

Mr Orrett, who was serving in France, wrote home shortly before the cessation of hostilities in November 1918. His letter combines the vein of patriotic optimism with the appalling reality with which this "war to end all wars" would forever be associated, and sounded an ominous note for the future which was not all that wide of the mark:

I am now sitting in a Boche's hut, which only yesterday morning was actually in Boche's possession. It is riddled with our shrapnel and from just a few hundred yards behind us is the glare of a famous town which he had been compelled to evacuate.

I am quite well and fit in spite of escapes so narrow that I can only be thankful to the bottom of my heart.

Of the officers who joined the Battalion when I did, two have been killed, gassed, several wounded, and two have gone down with trench fever. . .

Everything out here goes splendidly. And the news from other parts of the Front is most inspiring. Everyone is very cheery and hopes of an early victorious peace run high.

It is a case of "tails up" and the only fear expressed is lest the Boche should be let off too lightly and all the sacrifices of the past four years be thrown away through through an over eagerness for peace.

Let there be peace, but a peace that shall ensure peace, and not an artificial political peace which shall usher in another period of preparation for war. . .

The men out here are so splendid and sometimes one hears stories from some parts of the old country that the boys they have left to take the place of the men who are going through so much are getting out of hand, giving trouble at home and in school. If we had such lads at Solihull I should be ashamed ever to have been connected been with them; they would be failing do their bit in this struggle and be helping the Boche whom their fathers are fighting against . . .

In memoriam

Solihull's peace celebrations were spread throughout 1919.

July saw around 700 local children take part in festivities in a huge marquee laid out in Malvern Park, Punch and Judy providing evening entertainment.

Saturday, 13 September, saw the town give a rapturous welcome back for 400 Solihull servicemen. A column marched from Park Road school past the war shrine saluting the memory of the "Glorious Dead."

The rector concluded his speech at the subsequent dinner by reading a message from Field Marshall Earl Haig, commander in chief of the Allied forces:

I wish the ex-servicemen of Solihull a very happy welcome home, and look to them to work together now in peace for the good of our great country for which they fought so gallantly.

The village football team was revived for soldiers returning home and the cricket club, which had also been dormant during the war years, was also rekindled at its Broomfields headquarters.

Solihull, however, would never forget the nightmare that had dominated the decade and the sacrifices that the town had made.

A memorial to the fallen was erected in the square opposite the parish church and dedicated on Sunday, 19 June, 1921.

A procession of 500 parishioners moved from the gates of Malvern Park to the square, headed by the band of the Norton Homes.

The Lord Lieutenant, the Earl of Craven, unveiled the memorial before a firing party fired three volleys and buglers sounded the last post.

Dr Bernays read the names of the 103 inscribed on the memorial before the hymn *O God Our Help In Ages Past* was sung. Afterwards, the Bishop of Birmingham dedicated the monument which was handed over to the district council.

The more famous monument was the one erected at the traditional centre of England, Meriden village green, in 1921 in memory of Britain's cyclists who fell in armed combat.

It is still the scene of an annual service of remembrance that attracts cyclists from all over Britain on the nearest Sunday to May 22.

The end of another time-honoured custom. Dancing round the Maypole in Knowle ceased after this event in High Street opposite the Greswolde Hotel in 1919.

The guard of honour at the unveiling of Solihull war memorial in 1921.

At the MOUNT COTTAGE FARM - SHIRLEY. EX MONTE ALTO.

MOUNT COTTAGE FARM, near SHIRLEY.

FROM EASTER TO SEPTEMBER.

PIERROTS
(Saturday & Wednesday Afternoons).

THE ATHOL AND CECIL PIERROT VARIETY AND DRAMATIC COMPANY will give Three High-Class Performances every Saturday, commencing at 3-30 p.m., and every Wednesday, at 6-30 p.m.

GREAT VARIETY. ORIGINALITY. ABSOLUTE REFINEMENT.

QUARTETTES, TRIOS, CONCERTED NUMBERS, HUMOROUS MUSICAL AND DRAMATIC SKETCHES, Etc., Etc.

SACRED CONCERTS
Sunday Afternoons, at 3-30 p.m.

Opportunities will be given those attending the Concerts to contribute to the Vocal or Instrumental part of the Programme, thus affording latent talent the chance which is so often wanted.

Musical Director:
JACK ATHOL.

Stage Manager:
HAROLD H. HASTINGS.

All communications to be made to the Business Manager :—
FRED CECIL, The Cedars, Yardley, Birmingham.

MOUNT COTTAGE FARM, near SHIRLEY. (130 Acres.)

A Real Day in the Country for 1906. (No Charge for Admission.)

Dancing, Pierrots, Tennis, Bowls, Air-Gun Shooting, Swings, Donkeys, &c. Poultry Farm and Lovely Gardens. Cycle Shed.

CATERING FOR SCHOOL TREATS,
PICNICS AND EARLY CLOSING ASSOCIATION.

Two Covered Pavilions, each 60ft. long by 20ft. wide, to seat 560 Adults.

APPLY TO THE MANAGER FOR CATERING TERMS.

Chapter Three

A VICTORIOUS HOMECOMING
1920–29

Homes fit for heroes were promised to the servicemen returning from the front, yet in Solihull as everywhere else across the country there was a chronic shortage of housing.

Addison's Act of 1919 empowered local authorities to build municipal homes for letting, and the first council houses in Britain went up at Milton Green in Weston-super-Mare.

Houses for the better off were appearing in such numbers along Solihull's once-leafy lanes to the point that in 1920, councillors voiced proposals to reform the local authority as an urban rather than rural district council.

However, for those on labourer's wages there appeared to be even less accommodation available than before.

The RDC nevertheless decided to take a firm stand against people erecting 'temporary' wooden dwellings as makeshift homes without obtaining planning permission. At Solihull Petty Sessions in June 1920, John Hallgarth of Pritchett Street, Birmingham, and Frederick Goodwin of Knowle were each fined £2 for such misdeeds.

Both pleaded the housing shortage as an explanation for their action, and in November that year, Miss C. M. Griffiths of Handsworth was fined £2 for erecting a wooden building at the Mount in Cheswick Green. The court heard the argument that the government had been relaxing prewar planning restraints to cope with postwar situations.

The by-now disused pleasure gardens at the Mount were divided into plots of land and sold off to Birmingham folk as sites for weekend homes at £75 for 23,000 square yards . . . or 9d a yard.

Some of them, like the rich industrialists a few decades before, found that they liked the clean air and open space so much that they decided not to return.

A 300-home estate comprising wooden frame houses with tarpaulin roofs, not wholly dissimilar to a shanty town of the American deep south, with chicken coops, pigsties and allotment patches, all connected by a labyrinth of muddy roads, sprang up.

Sadly, many of these houses quickly became akin go the insanitary city slums that they replaced, and conditions caused local councillors a headache for the next half century.

One man told a visitor that he loved his job of opening up and emptying the cesspits that served the Mount homes.

The fumes were bad enough to overpower him, and even turned the coins in his pocket black.

But he was lucky – as he did not have a sense of smell!

A similar development was to be found at the Robin Hood allotments by the city boundary at Shirley, where caravan dwellers had moved among once-tidy brick bungalows, keeping pigs and living in conditions so cramped and squalid that a doctor once refused to visit a patient there.

Rather than finding any roof over their head, many returning war veterans were left with a life on the road.

Warwickshire's county vagrancy committee reported widespread distress among them through lack of suitable work, and a heavy increase in the number of tramps.

It was reported in October 1921 that the number of claims for proof relief throughout the county had rose by 20,324 over the previous quarter.

Early private health care?

The Solihull Board of Guardians, which was still responsible for poor relief in the district, in 1920 hit upon a new idea in its endless quest to get the workhouse to pay its way . . . by admitting patients other than paupers to its infirmary.

They hoped to open the "hospital" to paying members of the public, but the Ministry of health pointed out that it could not authorise the Guardians to give assistance to cases which they were not legally empowered to relieve.

The Ministry did, however, suggest that in view of the need to make use of the whole of the available accommodation, "temporary" arrangements might be made to rent out parts of the building to other public authorities in need of sick beds.

After the Guardians ceased to exist around 1926, responsibility for the workhouse passed to Warwickshire County Council, with the orphans, the mentally ill, tuberculosis sufferers and those suffering from other diseases removed to more suitable accommodation.

An overwhelming devotion

Diseases which can be easily treated in the 1990s brought fear and suffering to the Solihull population 70 years or so ago.

Beeches Farm in Beeches Lane, Olton, now known as Gospel Lane, was home to the Wall family, whose eldest son Fred died after developing sugar diabetes, for which there was then no cure.

His younger brother David then began to develop a burning thirst, one of the symptoms.

He would walk along the row of shops in Olton Hollow asking each shopkeeper for a drink of water to quench it.

One trader asked him why he did not drink water at his farm.

'I don't want my mother to know,' he replied.

David was outside the shops when he collapsed and was taken to hospital where he died – at a time when the insulin remedy was being developed in Canada.

Everyone in Olton was amazed at David's love for his mother.

Shortly after his death, the farmland was taken for a housing estate and his family was given a council house as a replacement.

Too free and easy

Life in Solihull was not all bleak and miserable in the postwar years and its pubs proved a big attraction from far and wide.

In August 1920, Solihull police put a block on "free and easy" concerts which had been held weekly at pubs in the centre.

Superintendent Carbis said that the "free and easies" had degenerated into "very undesirable assemblies" bringing rowdiness and drunkenness in their wake, and these Saturday night goings-on had become "a serious nuisance to the neighbourhood" with objectionable behaviour by numbers of young men and woman from "outside the village".

Frequent complaints had been received about rowdiness at Solihull railway station after closing time, he said.

No love lost

What started as a simple collision between two cars in Olton – by modern standards at least – opened a hornet's nest to public view.

Arthur Umfreville Harris, of the Colonnade Picture Theatre in Leamington Spa, brought an action for damages against George Edman of Copt Heath, who issued a counter claim.

Birmingham Assizes in July 1920 heard that Morris sounded his horn to pass a lorry in Warwick Road the previous December and was about to move clear when Edman's car came out of Dovehouse Lane and a collision occurred.

Morris said that not only had Edman been doing 20 miles an hour – but no horn had been sounded.

Under cross examination, Morris denied that he was "in love with" Mrs Greene, his secretary, who was a passenger in the car.

Yet after further questioning her admitted that she had recently been divorced – and he had been named as a co-respondent in the case.

It was then suggested that he had been paying more attention to her than the road at the time.

After Mrs Greene appeared as a witness and described Edman's speed as "terrific", the judge found in Morris' favour and dismissed the counter claim.

A first bypass demand

A plea to save picture-postcard villages from the ravages of motor traffic was made by the vicar of Knowle at a time when the car was taking over narrow lanes that had been designed only for pedestrians horse-drawn traffic.

Rev Thomas Downing, concerned that antique buildings might have to make way for modern roads, said in July 1923:

"If you were to stand with me at the vicarage gate on a Sunday evening in the summer and see the constant succession of motor cars dashing along as though it were a matter of life and death, if you were to know that these cars would soon be dashing through the village as though it belonged to them and that they could treat it anyhow, you would feel with me that something ought to be done to check the speed

of motor cars while they are going through an old village, especially on Sundays.

The policy of the new roadmakers is to sweep away everything that stands in the way, instead of trying to find new ways around the villages . . .

In the case of this place, some of the traffic might easily be diverted, the motorist would avoid a difficult gradient, would miss the village altogether, and would join the main road farther on . . ."

One Solihull bottleneck that remained notorious for most of the century received its first attempt at improvement in the mid twenties.

The Coventry Road near the Ye Old Malt Shovel public house at Stonebridge – said to be very narrow and dangerous – was widened, with a row of old cottages which obscured the view at the crossroads (later a roundabout) were demolished.

A "very important improvement" that would be appreciated by thousands of Midland motorists," commented the Birmingham Gazette.

Hurricane

Long before the greenhouse effect was blamed for freak weather, an "appalling hurricane" hit Solihull in October 1923.

Farm buildings at Silhill Hall were decimated and 42-year-old Patrick Murphy was killed when a barn collapsed on it as he sheltered inside.

A large Dutch barn was lifted off its foundations and carried for a hundred feet.

Cars were lifted off the road and horse-drawn carts were tipped over by the whirlwind as it tore through Sharmans Cross Road, Streetsbrook Road and Hermitage Road.

Fire water

We have previously seen how Solihull's fire brigade was praised for doing their best despite their severe limitations by modern standards.

Events around Christmas 1925, however, proved that they were also capable of doing their worst and causing a major scandal in still sleepy Solihull.

A fierce Arctic storm raged from 9 p.m. on Saturday, 19 December, until noon the following day, leaving snow four inches deep.

At Cow Hayes Farm in Ravenshaw, the owner, widow Lady Catherine Reynolds, was woken up at 4.30 a.m. on the Monday morning by screaming from the house maids. The house was ablaze.

Smoke filled the bedroom when she opened the door, and she dashed back to snatch her four-year-old daughter Kitty from her cot.

Prevented from going down the stairs by a wall of flame, Lady Reynolds pulled down a curtain and told Kitty to hang on tight . . . before lowering her from a first-floor window, before jumping herself.

The fire had burned out the telephone – SOL 159 – so a neighbour rushed to Solihull to summon the fire brigade as the property became a raging inferno, destroying valuable furniture and Lady Reynolds's late solicitor husband's priceless library and collection of photographs.

Lady Reynolds and Kitty were taken to the George Hotel.

Kitty who was living on the Isle of Man in the 1990s, still had vivid recollections of the awful day: "I remember my ice-cold feet as I stood on the little bit of flat roof outside the bedroom window while Mother unhooked a thick curtain to wrap me in and break my fall.

"I remember the roar of the flames as we stood on the lawn watching the house being engulfed, and then the relief as the maids came safely around the side of the house."

And a district council official who visited the scene received the shock of his life.

For several of the firemen were blind drunk.

After damping down the flames, the crew found that the wine cellar was relatively unscathed – and raided it.

Not only had they drunk several bottles at the scene but also taken many home with them.

The council held an inquiry – behind closed doors.

It was said on the crew's behalf that they had been weary and cold and gave in to the temptation of free liquor.

Lady Renolds denied inviting them to have a drink or salvage the cellar contents.

The two officers in charge were asked to resign and seven firemen were sacked. The brigade was then handed over to the control of Mr Rowland Bragg who did the job voluntarily for a year.

Pictures that move

Plans for Solihull's first cinema were laid in 1922 when a Mr Clifford proposed building one in Poplar Road. However it was to be another four years before Ye Arden Picture House opened in High Street, next to the Royal Oak.

Plush gold upholstery and potted palm plants welcomed the first customers to the world of silent fantasy and glamour.

An orchestra provided romantic melodies to accompany the action on the silver screen. Topping the bill on the first night was *The Man On The Box* starring Syd Chaplin.

Thirteen staff were employed, the highest paid being the band leader who picked up £6 a week, twice a much as the manager, while electricity was supplied by an oil generator.

Solihull's rector Rev Harvey Brooks, who retired in 1926 handing over office to his son-in-law Rev Charles Wormald after 32 years, commented:

Above all there is the drama of human life, and here is the thing which is of vast importance to our Solihull community. For the sake of our moral welfare, we ask the proprietors to exercise the greatest care in choosing the films to be displayed.

We don't want pictures which stimulate wrong imaginations. We don't want to be forced to watch the details of moral lawlessness.

We don't want unwholesome suggestions. We do want to be amused and educated and we want to take our young boys and girls with us.

It became the first in the Midlands outside Birmingham to show talking pictures, the first being *Showboat*. "Talkies" did not reach Ye Arden until 1930 when Victor McLaglan and Edmund Lowe starred in *The Cock-Eyed World*.

Malvern Park

Another major addition to the embryonic Solihull townscape in 1926 was Malvern Park.

Although the 18th century parkland had been used to hold major events on in the village calendar for many years, the council wanted to acquire open space where local children could safely play.

The expanding "village" – where there were currently plans to build more than 200 homes – reinforced this need.

A bid by the council to buy nearly 17 acres of the park and provide a recreation ground with a £4,000 loan from the Ministry of Health was the subject of a public inquiry the previous November.

Councillors voted by a majority of one to buy the land, while Shirley Ratepayers member Dr Coole Neale said that Shirley and Olton had a more urgent need than Solihull for such facilities.

The park – the first in Solihull – was opened on Saturday, 10 July, by Mrs Maurice Davis, who flung the entrance gates wide open so that a procession of children marched through in military-fashion to take possession of their new playground.

Mr W. T. Horton, chairman of the open spaces recreation grounds committee, said that he hoped before long other local recreation grounds would be opened.

His hopes were soon fulfilled, for on 10 September 1927, Shirley's recreation ground, later known as Shirley Park was opened by Dr Neale, on a site behind the Saracen's Head, amidst much fanfare, a massive street procession and great jubilation. Part of the site had formerly been occupied by a riding school where annual horse shows were held.

Local firemen take part in the Shirley Carnival procession in 1927, when the town's recreation ground was opened. The carnival was a major event in the calendar, attracting up to 30,000 people. Abandoned in 1960, the event was revived 20 years later when carnival queen Elaine Gordon performed the opening ceremony.

A Bizarre Fatality

An unusual fatality occurred at Solihull yesterday, the victim being a 17-year-old domestic servant, Phyllis Lilian Chadwick, of Brook Hill, Shustoke, who was employed by Mr Sperryn, of Hampton Grange.

Miss Chadwick went into the kitchen about 11 o'clock and placed her hands on the mantlepiece, which suddenly fell away from the wall, pinning her to the floor. The girl was badly injured about the head and died before medical assistance could be secured.

(Birmingham Gazette, 3 August 1926)

Wired for sound

Fears for the despoiling of Solihull's "leafy glories" were sounded when the Post Office made plans to expand the telephone network into the rural fringe.

Before a Birmingham County Court judge in 1926, Solihull RDC argued firmly against overhead wires on telegraph poles in the countryside and said that cables should instead be buried underground.

The wires in question were earmarked to run from Widney Manor Road in Solihull to Tilehouse Road in Knowle.

The Post Office argued that the cost of underground cable would be more than double even if the council dug and filled a trench at their own expense, while the small amount of subscribers in a rural area did not justify it.

The council said that overhead wires would "spoil the leafy beauty of the lanes" by causing the trees to be cut, and its surveyor, Albert Currall, stated that the area was part of the old Forest of Arden and the Selborne Society had asked him to assist in the preservation of the trees and undergrowth.

Evidence was given of "the frequent disturbance of telephone efficiency where overhead wires were carried near trees, of the annoyance of the constant buzzing of the wires and of their unsightliness."

The judge asked the Postmaster General to reconsider the case in the light of the council's representations.

An educational upheaval

A proposal from the council's director of education caused no little consternation among the St Alphege clergy in 1927.

The local authority wanted to build a new Central Council School to cater for all children over the age of 11 who currently attended the elementary schools.

Rector Wormald had grave misgivings:

Definite Church teaching will not be given to our children between the ages of 11 and 15, and even though an undenominational syllabus of religious instruction is adopted by the local authority, there is to be no pledge that the teacher believes what he teaches.

The children attending this new school will come from Solihull, Shirley and Olton, with an ever-increasing population. In a few years' time, doubtless additions will be required . . .

Local hero

A stirring story of a Solihull man's heroism in the shark-infested waters of the west coast of Africa has just reached Birmingham.

Mr E. T. Davis of the Elms, Widney Lane, who is at present serving on the Elder Dempster motor vessel Adda has just been awarded the Liverpool Shipwreck and Humane Society's silver lifesaving medal and illuminated vote of thanks in recognition of his action of outstanding gallantry.

It appears that at about 7.30 a.m. on 3 January when the Adda was about 200 miles from Sierra Leone on her outward voyage, one of the second-class passengers, Mr W. Butcher, by some means fell into the sea.

Before the boat was launched, second officer Lovegreen dived overboard an on reaching the body was himself in danger of losing his life.

Third Officer Davis then dived into the seat and swam with a lifebuoy to Butcher's body which he succeeded in placing inside the buoy.

Mr Davis then assisted his fellow officer who was in an exhausted condition.

(Birmingham Gazette, 8 February 1927)

The queen of all mothers.

For most villagers in the twenties, a royal visit was the big event of the decade – something that may escape modern-day Silhillians when trips by major and minor members of the Windsor clan to the National Exhibition Centre and other major attractions are a fairly frequent occurrence.

August 1927 saw Queen Mary, wife of George V, staying at Castle Bromwich Hall as guest of the Dowager Countess of Bradford, as part of a summer tour of the Midlands. She had, a Princess May, planted a tree in the grounds there some years before.

Royal fever reached such a pitch that the rector of Castle Bromwich issued tickets to parishioners so that they would not be crowded out of the church during Her Majesty's attendance on the Sunday.

On 24 August, she delighted the inhabitants of Knowle who lined Warwick Road to cheer her as she was driven to Packwood house, then home of Mr Graham Baron Ash.

The Queen said that she was "fascinated" by the country mansion with its fine Tudor interior.

"The most wonderful house I have seen", exclaimed a member of the Queen's party, and Her Majesty smiled assent. She expressed herself as particularly charmed by the religious yew garden.

After inspecting the house and gardens, the Queen and her party were entertained to tea by Mr Baron Ash and his sister Mrs Mellor in a former cow byre, which has been transformed into what experts assert is the most perfect copy of a Tudor great hall in existence. Silver plate from the royal collection of the Kings of Hanover were used . . .

A delightful incident occurred as the Queen, with obvious reluctance, left this house of art and antique treasures.

Little Bunty Mellor, the eight-year-old nice of Mr Ash, who was born on

Armistice Day, presented Her Majesty with a bouquet. "It is perfectly charming," said the Queen.

"Yes, Majesty," said the child. "Mother made it. So of course it would be".

(Birmingham Gazette, 24 August 1927)

Our prize goal

The Solihull parish magazine ran a competition in 1928. A prize was to be awarded for the best answer to the question, "What is most wanted in Solihull?"

Reader Mr A. G. Roberts came up trumps:

What we should like and what we shall get,
Are probably far removed,
One thinks of diverse wonderful ways,
Of having our village improved,
Things that may gladden the critical eye,
To our aesthetic senses appealing,
But might I suggest a foundation for all?
We want the "Community Feeling".

A worthy aim indeed – at a time when new suburban-style roads eating into virgin pastures in Solihull, Shirley and Olton, modern facilities were being demanded by the new residents, and the "village" at the core of the district council was soon to undergo a major metamorphosis which would see it throw off its ancient predominantly rural identity forever.

Chapter Four

AN URBAN FLEDGLING
1930–39

There had been no stopping the growth of either Birmingham or Solihull as the twenties drew to a close.

A final decision had to be made about the way forward – whether the "village" Solihull was to accept its new "town" identify and the responsibilities that went with it, or be swallowed up by the city.

In May 1930 Solihull RDC. heard that Warwickshire County Council would accede to its request to become an urban authority, provided that it gave up the entirely rural parishes on its fringe.

Solihull would have to give up Hockey Heath, Foresaw Heath, Packwood, Baddesley Clinton, Lapworth, Balsall, Barston and parts of Knowle and Elmdon, the eastern parishes being absorbed by a new Coleshill-based Meriden RDC.

At least one area was to be dragged screaming into adjacent Stratford-upon-Avon RDC against everyone's wishes:

> *Referring to Tanworth, Coun W E Ward said they had nursed the infant until it was a lusty child. In a short time, Tanworth would be very wealthy . . . and Solihull . . . could not have the parish when it became a valuable possession. Tanworth was getting electricity, and shortly would be provided with water. The next thing would be sewerage . . .*
>
> (WCN)

Solihull's bid for a comprise with the parishes outside the new urban district formed a "rump" rural district council, possibly with Knowle as its centre, was rejected.

The Minister of Health formally granted Solihull urban district council status from 1 April 1932 – minus those rural outposts. Captain David Gee, chairman of the RDC, said that like good losers "they are prepared to make the best of it".

The RDC met for the last time in the boardroom of the Poor Law Institution. Capt Gee concluded his farewell speech by saying that urbanisation "must be an advantage" to Solihull, and eventually the district might even become a borough!

New £19,000 council offices replaced the Public Hall in Poplar Road as the previous headquarters had become too small.

From this point onwards, urbanisation threatened to run riot, with housebuilding engulfing more and more farmland.

Council surveyor R Dunn reported in 1936 that an "abnormal" rate of development was being maintained, with a 52.7 per cent increase in the number of houses in the district in just four years, and many more new roads being laid out.

Solihull was now the second largest urban district in England, and Capt Gee's prediction was echoed within a few years when calls were sounded for the next step to be made – "upgrading" to a full-blown municipal borough – possibly named "Solihull and Shirley."

The new wave of expansion saw worsening friction between Solihull and its dissatisfied younger upstart to the west – with a never-ending stream of complaints that the latter was being maltreated or plainly ignored.

Annexation

Shirley abuts on to the city boundary . . . the residents of Shirley have all their interests in Birmingham; they earn their living there; they shop there; they have to go there for their amusement . . . Shirley people have no interest whatsoever in Solihull.

There is no direct connection between the two places except by the occasional 'bus...annexation to Birmingham would mean main drainage, better roads, cheaper electricity, better travelling facilities by tram and omnibus . . . Solihull regards Shirley in pretty much the same light . . . Shirley is a suburb of Birmingham except in name.

Now we want to see it develop on modern and progressive lines, an and have done with the old haphazard come-and-go-as-you-please methods . . . which have given us the present petrol-pump-cum-eating-house-cum-pub kind of village, which Shirley is today....

The letter from "HCL of Shirley" to the Warwick County News in 1930 summarised an acrimonious debate that would occupy council matters for much of the decade.

The question of a city takeover of Shirley was debated again in 1937, when some senior members of the local residents association came out in favour.

Most local councillors, however, would not hear of it, and won support from city councillor Bernard Alderson, who represented Handsworth ward but lived in Solihull.

Birmingham does not want to annexe Shirley or Olton. When the annexation of Sheldon and Castle Bromwich was under consideration, the inclusion of Shirley was mentioned, but the proposal was not even discussed. Birmingham is now quite big enough . . .

If Shirley became part of the city it would lose its identity . . . if it joined the family circle in Birmingham it would become one of a number of children each asking for special favours. They cannot all be satisfied however loud they plead for more amenities . . .

Solihull has only two growing children, but Birmingham has several. Shirley must have patience, and when it feels the "growing pains" and asks for more improvements, it must realise that they can only come gradually . . .

The slums of Solihull

"Improvements" had indeed been needed in many parts of Shirley and surrounding areas for many year.

While Solihull's steady expansion had stabilised its image of affluence and luxury, the outer districts' ramshackle dwellings built in the aftermath of the war years had become a major embarrassment. Apart from the Mount and the Robin Hood allotment

Workmen moving the cobbles from High Street, Solihull, in the 1930s. Sixty years later, it was the turn of the tarmac to go – as block paving came in with the major pedestrianisation scheme which closed High Street to motor traffic in the nineties.

"Des Res" in Fisher's Drive, Dickens Heath, showing the type of temporary shanty dwelling that caused much consternation at various sites around the district between the wars.
Luxury homes were later built on many such plots in Fisher's Drive.

site, leaky wooden eyesore hutments in Tythebarn Lane, Shirley, were also described as slums.

There, inhabitants washed in tubs of water collected from the nearby Stratford-upon-Avon Canal and carried drinking water 150 yards.

Stories of a then-scandalous £350 a year ground rent for shacks in Prince of Wales Lane, Solihull Lodge, were also told. One resident, Mrs J Bird, said she would gladly exchange it for a council house, having suffered pneumonia twice in eight years.

Even the new brick council houses came under fire for living conditions. Those in Tythebarn Lane, for instance, had no gas, electricity or kitchen fire grates.

Eight people lived in a two-roomed house in Longmore Lane, Shirley, which had one bed and no water. The filthy state of the house was described as shocking and appalling. "I have never conceived anything so appalling in the midst of a community which prides itself on its progressive ways," wrote a weekly news reporter.

In February 1931, Birmingham County Court heard that Charles Docker, who rented pigsties at Francis Villa in Haslucks Green Road, Shirley, actually slept in them after the adjoining house in which he had been a tenant had been sold. Bailiffs turned him out, but they had no jurisdiction over the garden, and so he made up a single trestle bed and slept among his 40 hogs.

The purchaser of the property refused to take it up in the circumstances, and the court ordered Docker and his pigs to leave within three weeks.

Shirley's Dr Neale said that residents had been plagued by refuse tips for some time and there had been a lowering of the health.

It was suggested that a tip should be placed in one of the better parts of Solihull, but instantly there came a petition from residents of the neighbourhood, the weekly news reported.

One particular tip in Haslucks Green Road was the principal source of outrage as well as home to "thousands" of rats.

Coun F J Ward credited rats with some degree of intelligence – and said that if holes leading to the tip were blocked, they would realise that someone was after them, and soon move away.

Lighting up time

Electric lighting with all its benefits came to the streets of villages like Hampton-in-Arden.

However one local, Thomas Russell, of Belle Vue terrace, remained somewhat unconvinced, after workmen left wires hanging too low over a grass footpath.

Irritated by this, he hacked them down, and landed before Solihull Police Court in May 1930.

J Bearman, a jointer employed by Calendars Cable and Construction Co Ltd., said the defendant came to him and said he was going to cut down the wires . . . defendant then went away, but soon returned with a hammer and trowel, with which he cut down the wires.

He threatened to cut witness's nose and elbow off if he came near him.

Russell was fined £1 with £2 costs.

Early life in the fast lane

The speed limit for lorries using Coventry Road in Sheldon in 1931 was . . . a breathtaking 16 miles an hour, and local police went to extremes to enforce it, magistrates at Solihull heard.

The town's police court heard in December that a trap covering nine miles was set up and netted lorrydriver Robert Miller from Coseley, who was tearing down at a wicked 25mph.

Defending solicitor W T Horton told the bench that "strong efforts were being made to raise the speed limit of this class of vehicle to twenty miles an hour". Miller was fined 50s.

Traffic police in Solihull again came under fire in 1937 when they introduced a new method of catching speeding motorists – a worsening problem as car ownership rose. Speeding cases before the town's magistrates soared from 12 to 50 in a week. The scheme involved driving *in front* of a offending vehicle rather than following it, and using fixed points on the driver's mirror to see whether its speed was increasing.

Midland Red bus driver John Lane from Stafford, accused of doing 42mph in a 30 zone in Hockley Heath, said he had been concentrating more on the unmarked car in front than his speedometer because the vehicle would not get out of the way and gave no signals.

He was fined 10s, despite his lawyer's pleas that the tactic was "very unreasonable, unreliable and might be a little dangerous".

Reginald Massey of Derby alleged that the officers' car tried to cut out in front of him six times and said:" I thought it was some mad-headed devil in the car but it turned out to be the police." Fine – 20s.

Edward Stokoe, of Handsworth, said that the road from Knowle to Solihull was so dark that he thought it was derestricted landed him with a 10s penalty.

"I say the car won't do it!" said Harold Powell, of Stratford Road, Shirley – also fined 20s. for speeding.

The polite society

> It was revealed at Henley Police Court that after an accident between two cars, (on Stratford Road, Hockley Heath) which caused one of them to skid across the road, mount the grass verge, and turn upside down, and the other to swing around and fall on its side, the drivers of the respective vehicles, who were both uninjured, made no complaints, merely enquiring after each other's physical condition and exchanging addresses.
>
> (WCN, November 1930)

Progress in education

New residents meant that new schools were needed and fast, despite the previous forebodings of local vicars.

Malvern Hall, the mansion built by Humphrey Greswold in 1640 and painted several times by John Constable opened as a girls' secondary school in 1931, the fees being £11 11s per annum.

It catered for pupils aged 11–18, though you could get in at 10 if you were sufficiently bright.

The fees included stationery, but pupils had to buy their own textbooks, and there was a small annual subscription for games.

Scholarships could be won to earn free places and the first headmistress was Miss F M Forster.

Meanwhile, the new 520-pupil senior council school serving Solihull, Olton and Shirley, built at a cost of nearly £20,000, opened at Sharmans Cross with Mr Orrett as headmaster.

With its gym, woodwork shops, library and playing fields, it was described as the best in Warwickshire.

However, a less enthusiastic reception was given by Tidbury Green residents to the area's new infants school, set up in a temporary buildings likened to a wooden "army hut".

A modern fire station at last

Solihull's fire brigade was finally yanked into the modern world in 1932 when it was decided to close outlying substations at Olton, Shirley and Hockley Heath, and consolidate resources on a central site in Streetsbrook Road – while buying a supplementary £910 engine in case of emergencies.

Shirley fire station, situated in part of a shoemaker's shed, was said to be "the joke of all who passed", and the doors had not been opened for several years.

Four of its firemen did not even have uniforms.

Faithful to the end

> So many people attended Knowle church to pay their last tribute to the late Canon T W Downing, vicar of the parish for 31 years, that all the mourners could not be accommodated in the church . . .
>
> Among those who followed to the graveside, where the Rev J W Sharp, of St Philip's, Dorridge, was Rob, the vicar's Aberdeen terrier, to which he was very much attached.

(WCN, 1932)

Getting the edge in a competitive world

Birmingham manufacturer John Guthrie Southerland was determined to win a £10,000 business contract in Brighton.

Nothing was going to stop him . . . not even a 60 miles an hour express train at Knowle & Dorridge station.

Southerland, of Kelvedon, Lode Lane, was dismayed when, after reaching the station to board the London-bound train, he sent his chauffeur home – and then found that it was not going to stop.

So he stood on the tracks frantically waving his hat as the express hurtled towards him, Solihull magistrates heard.

He did not jump out of the way of the engine until the very last moment, the court was told.

The bench heard that Southerland had arranged to negotiate with Brighton & Hove Corporation about the contract that very day.

When the station clerk refused to stop the train, he pleaded that the contract would mean an extra £2,000 a year to the GWR in goods traffic.

Scotsman Southerland then begged a signalman to halt the express, and when he also refused, the businessman said: "If you don't, I shall".

He then walked on to the line.

After the train screeched to a half, Southerland calmly got on to the train.

He was interviewed by Inspector Haines of the GWR – and told him that the £5 maximum fine was nothing compared to the potential lost business.

Magistrates fined him for trespassing on the railway and also ordered him to pay ten guineas costs.

But he won the contract. (WCN 1932)

Nothing left

The Catholic church of St George, Dorridge, was burned completely to the ground and everything in it lost by a disastrous fire which broke out at four o'clock.

So fiercely did the fire rage that the whole building was completely demolished in three-quarters of an hour despite the efforts of Solihull fire brigade and willing helpers from the village.

There is something poignant in the fact that catholics at Dorridge have worked untiringly to build their church and had almost paid off the debt on the building.

The fire was believed to have been started by a fused alter lamp.

(WCN, February 1934)

First carnival queen

Solihull's first carnival queen was Mary Grace Bragg, aged 17, whose father nominated her for the contest in 1932, which was held at the Stork hotel in Birmingham.

An ox was roasted at the event and Mary's fiance George bought the first piece for a guinea.

The crowning took place outside St Alphege church and Mary had to place a wreath on the war memorial afterwards.

The carnival procession featured carriages and a stage coach drawn by four horses.

Shirley's superb facilities.

Despite the feelings among residents that Shirley was Solihull's Cinderella suburb, it received four state-of-the-art facilities in the 1930s.

The first was Shirley Stadium, a magnificent non-league soccer pitch on land between Bills Lane and Shirley Park, developed by local contractor George Featherstone.

It become home to Shirley Town FC, hitherto members of the grass-roots Sparkbrook League, whose new facilities allowed them to springboard into the prestigious Birmingham League alongside Bromsgrove Rovers, Tamworth, Redditch and the "A" teams of Aston Villa, West Bromwich Albion and Coventry City.

The stadium was the venue for many big events and in July 1937 hosted a women's soccer international which saw England beat France 13–0. It was sold off for housing after world War Two.

A second facility was an open air swimming pool complete with dance hall at a site now in Hurdis Road.

Opened in a blaze of publicity in June 1936, Shirley Lido was nota commercial success and closed three years later, later being converted into the headquarters of Simmons & Sons Ltd paper merchants and, more recently, partially bulldozed and the site used for housing.

Another new amenity was a free library, installed in a council-owned property in School Road with 2,000 books, despite a county branch library at nearby Church House earlier failing due to a lack of volunteers.

Shirley also received its own cinema in Stratford Road, the Odeon, opened on 15 April 1935.

Converted to a bingo hall in the late seventies, a Safeway supermarket now stands on the site.

New hostelries

The booming population and increase in motor traffic led to demands for bigger and better public houses.

In Knowle, the licence of the ancient White Swan pub was switched to the new Lyndon pub in Olton before the former was demolished.

Much of the fabric of the White Swan was taken down and stored at a secret location, a field behind Haycocks Farm in Bakers Lane, Knowle, with the vain hope of re-erecting it at another site, Bricks, beams and slates were decades later used in the conversion of a one-up one-down house in the lane into Silica, a spacious luxury home, by electrician Donald Shaw.

Knowle licensees saw red when plans were announced in 1935 to convert Victorian Chadwick Manor into a guest house complete with facilities for fishing, boating, tennis, riding and golf, aimed at the "motoring community".

A drinks licence was granted after it was stressed that it would not compete with local pubs like the Black Boy. After decades as an hotel, the manor was converted to luxury flats in the 1980s.

The licence of the Union Inn, which stood at the corner of Union Road and Stratford road in Shirley, was transferred to new premises a mile away, the Three Maypoles pub in Tanworth Lane, built on the site of a cider mill. That pub became the Pickwick in the 1970s, and in 1996 was refurbished as the Cheswick Green Inn, even though it lies more than a mile from the place.

Plans to close the canalside Anchor Inn in Solihull Lodge and transfer the licence to a new pub at the junction of Haslucks Green Road and Colebrook Road, eventually named the Colebrook, divided the community, with petitions both for and against.

Meanwhile, as police figures showed an increase in drunkenness cases in 1936, Shirley vicar the Rev J Emlyn Jones procrastinating at the "menace to our peace" that such licence transfers caused by attracting more city revellers purely for drinking purposes.

The following year, Solihull justices refused a summer extension of opening hours from 10pm to 10.30pm after the clergy opposed it.

Shirley Stadium – the magnificent prewar non-league soccer venue next to Shirley Park built by George Featherstone and home to Shirley Town, whose players included the young future Birmingham City and England goalkeeper Gil Merrick. It was sold for housing after the war, but a team using the name still plays in Tilehouse Lane, Whitlocks End.

The Square in Knowle sometime before 1936, when the White Swan pub (the half timbered building next to the Red Lion, right) was demolished and its licence switched to the new Lyndon pub.

Home life, Mr J W Jessop (for the opposition) said, would suffer through the extension.

It would bring the father home later at night to his wife and children, and would probably wake the children up. This was not to be desired just at a time when the Government was spending two million pounds for the increase of physical fitness in children.

(WCN)

Factories

Shirley did not want factories in its backyard at any price.

That was the message from a packed meeting of the local residents association chaired by Eric Bowes, in response to another conflict with "posh" Solihull in 1936. Unfortunately it fell on deaf ears.

The protest was ignited by Solihull's latest town planning scheme which allocated 300 acres of land for industrial purposes in Shirley.

Some councillors said that factory sites were good for the district, and, according to the Warwick County News, "with wonderful self denial", had insisted on Shirley taking the lot.

When, however, Mr L M Cook wanted to erect a building in the back garden of his home in Dingle Lane, Solihull, to accommodate up to six ladies dressmaking, much anger was expressed by neighbours including Lady Edith Bird of Tudor Grange. Contemptuously described as a factory, planning permission for it was refused.

"That Shirley has more to grumble about than Solihull Council seems to think is a freely-expressed opinion in the village, now more like a town, which for years Solihull has thought of as a running sore always festering – and most unpleasantly – near a select residential area," wrote the weekly news.

Among the first factories to locate to the new Cranmore industrial estate were Carrs Paper Ltd., the Co-operative Wholesale Society and the Deloro Smelting and Refining Co Ltd.

Was Shirley set to become another Tyseley, it was asked.

The date stays the same

Street parties that ecstatically celebrated the silver jubilee of George V in 1935 all over the district soon faded from memory with the announcement of his death the following February.

Solihull was said to be "a deserted village" with an atmosphere more sombre than the sad gloom of Armistice Day.

Around 1,000 pupils from Solihull School and Solihull High School for girls attended a service at St Alphege. A hundred chairs had to be loaned by the George Hotel when the subsequent Sunday service was packed to overflowing with mourners.

Everyone prepared for his son to be crowned as Edward VIII, and preparations began to celebrate Coronation Day. However, a nationwide news blackout on subsequent events kept everyone in the dark about his intentions to marry divorcee Wallis Simpson.

Prime Minister Stanley Baldwin acted to suppressed any adverse press comment, fearing a national scandal, and was backed by newspaper magnate Lord Beaverbrook, who persuaded his Fleet Street rivals also not to run the story for an amazing ten months . . . despite it being plastered over the front page of every newspaper in Europe and America. So much for a democracy with a "free press.

When details of Edward's abdication became known, the public immediately accepted George VI as his replacement – and coronation celebrations went ahead . . . on the original date.

An eye for a beauty

A dark-eyed beauty who described herself as a French Canadian and who gave an address in Carlyle Road, Edgbaston, stood in the dock at Solihull charged with stealing 37 by means of a trick.

Her name was Susy Staveson . . . she was dressed in the picturesque costume of the gipsy and she wore her coal-black hair in plaits over her breast.

Mr C C Ladds, who prosecuted, told an extraordinary story. Staveson called at the Shirley surgery of Mr G H Bennett-Edwards in company with another woman. Staveson had said that she wanted some extractions, and the dentist advised her that two should be removed. She said she would come again tomorrow.

Before she went, however, she asked the dentist if she might see the palm of his hand in order to tell him his fortune.

She asked him for a penny and a handkerchief, and these he handed to her. Then she asked Mr Edwards' nurse to go out of the room, saying that what she had to say was not for her ears.

She gave him the coin and the handkerchief and then asked if he had any paper money.

He handed her a pound note and she made certain passes with it saying words and placing it under Mr Edwards' chin and in places on his chest.

He took her into the hall where the safe was situated, and he took from it a bundle of 27 £1 notes and handed them to her.

She said: "I am going to multiply them" and . . . went through the same motions as before. Afterwards she handed back what the dentist thought was the complete bundle of notes.

She asked him to give her some money for luck, and suggested three or four pounds. He refused, but gave her 1s, and she went away.

About half an hour later Mr Edwards became rather suspicious . . . and found that seven pounds were missing.

The dark-eyed beauty was fined £10.

Taking to the air

Aeroplanes were a damn nuisance.

That was the informed opinion of Councillor W C Hook, who discovered that the Wolverhampton Aviation Company had leased land in Longmore Lane, Shirley, for holding pleasure flights in 1930.

On Sunday they were flying over the houses, and it was one considerable rattle all the time. He did not think it should be allowed.

The vicar of Shirley had told him that he would be pleased if the aeroplanes did not pass over the church during divine service.

The clerk said he had looked through the county council's by-law dealing with noise, but he could find nothing dealing with aeroplanes.

Practically everything else was mentioned – even loudspeakers.

Whether they enjoyed the company's pleasure flights or not, Shirley residents were understandably horrified by a report from a Birmingham "council correspondent" who wrote in the Warwick County News in December that year:

We decided . . . to have a scheme prepared for the establishment of a muncipal airport at Shirley. We made the decision on a minimum of information and without any discussion.

We were not informed where the site of the proposed aerodrome is. We were told that the total cost would be in the neighbourhood of £70,000 and that Sir Alan Cobham had been consulted about the possibility.

Shirley residents were not even mentioned in the discussion – they are not city ratepayers.

The scheme haunted Shirley at various times in the decade – and other sites at Hillfield Farm, Shelley Green and Earlswood were also seriously considered , although Sir Alan, a distinguished wartime RAF pilot, whose motto was "Make the Skyways Britain's Highways," revealed that he had surveyed another site at Elmdon . . .

Meanwhile, air pageants at Widney Manor with aerobatics and parachute displays and 20-minute passenger flights organised by Sir Alan proved enormously popular – to the point that "few people were left in Solihull and the surrounding villages".

Stratford Road, Shirley, during the terrible winter of 1947. Fourteen inches of snow fell in 27 hours during March, when Stratford Road at Hockley Heath and Warwick Road at Chadwick End were blocked, buses were trapped in six-foot drifts overnight, Tanworth-in-Arden was cut off and even the Isolation Hospital at Catherine-de-Barnes became isolated several times.

A display of aerial bombing . . . called the Battle of the Flowers . . . followed . . . and in bombing a honeymooning couple and their chaurffeur, the pilot display a skill that had to be seen to be believed.

As the car drove across the flying ground the pilot swooped down at an incredible speed and dropped a "bomb" on the car.

When the car was "on fire" and its occupants were running about the field, the pilot turned his attention to them and it was seldom that he missed his objective . . .

Popular with everyone, yes – apart from two Birmingham members of the British Anti-War Movement who ended up before magistrates after repeatedly chalking pacifist slogans in Poplar Road in protest at the event.

Elmdon was eventually chosen as the site for Birmingham's airport, and was opened amidst much fanfare on 8 July 1939 by the Duchess of Kent...whose plans to fly back to London from it were thwarted by bad weather and she had to take the train instead.

Yet despite this initial failure, it was already clear that space for extended runways to cater for new bigger airliners would soon be needed, and the airport authorities bought up more land in readiness.

The Birmingham Evening Despatch lamented the loss of the "quiet spot between Bickenhill and the village of Marston Green" akin to "a parkland of graceful alder and or gnarled and battered oaks, of holly and of ash and fair Warwickshire's weeds".

Yet again – *the symbol of our age, speed, and the price man is prepared to pay for it, have combined to destroy our one-time peacefulness and solitide.*

But at least it did not end up in Shirley.

SOLIHULL CARNIVAL
TO-DAY
SATURDAY, MAY 6th

BIGGER! BRIGHTER! BETTER!

PAGEANT OF KING ARTHUR AND THE KNIGHTS OF
THE ROUND TABLE
CROWNING OF CARNIVAL QUEEN 2-45 p.m.
FANCY DRESS PARADE & DECORATED PROCESSIONS
JAZZ BAND COMPETITION
BARREL ORGAN COMPETITION
VALUABLE PRIZES

ROLL UP AND JOIN IN THE PROCESSIONS

GREAT OLD ENGLISH FAIR
IN THE NEW CARNIVAL FIELD AT
BROOMFIELDS, SOLIHULL
ADMISSION 2d.

BUY A PROGRAMME AND FOLLOW THE EVENTS—
YOU MAY WIN A B.S.A. BICYCLE
WIN A NEW AUSTIN EIGHT

GRAND PEACE CELEBRATION
SHIRLEY LIDO
MONDAY, OCTOBER 17th
8.30 p.m. — 1 a.m.
ADMISSION - - 2/6

Whole of proceeds for Benevolent Fund of Shirley Branch of the British

Chapter Five

WORLD WAR TWO
1939–45

For most Silhillians, like their counterparts throughout Britain, the big question in 1938 was not was there going to be another war with Germany, but how soon.

Neville Chamberlain's proclamation of "peace in our time" reassured few. "Grand Peace Celebrations" were held at the Shirley Lido in October 1938, but basic preparations for war were by then well underway in Solihull.

Air raid wardens had been mobilised and 500 of them attached to the Solihull sub division addressed by their commander at a meeting in September 1938 heard that the town was a danger area because of its proximity to Birmingham, the great manufacturing hub of Britain, and a prime bomber target.

Gas masks for Solihull children were already on order – some coming in a Mickey Mouse design, while babies had a portable chamber.

A bomb-proof concrete roof six inches thick to protect pupils at the new Lode Heath secondary school was installed during its construction in summer 1938.

The roof could withstand incendiary bombs but not high explosives and it was said to be the first school to offer such protection.

A national service recruiting drive held by Solihull ARP over a week in Shirley Odeon in May 1939 saw services including the Auxiliary Air Force, the Shirley Searchlight Battery, air wardens, first aid parties, rescue and decontamination groups, the British Red Cross and the Wythall Balloon Barrage seeking recruits in earnest. Warwickshire rates went up by a penny to pay for the cost of the new civil defence.

A green field site in Lode Lane was chosen as the site for the Rover Meteor shadow factory producing engines for Hercules aircraft, while the Austin company had its Aero Works at Elmdon airport, where pilots were trained, initially in outdated Tiger Moths.

The concept of shadow factories was for production to be run in tandem with a factory elsewhere: if one was bombed, the other would still churn out vital parts for the same production line. The British Small Arms company built a shadow factory at Wilde's Farm in Marshall Lake Road.

In August, the UDC approved the building of public air raid shelters without waiting for Home Office approval.

The ARP's nerve centre was established in the basement below the Council House, reinforced with concreted steel girders and a steel door to prevent poison gas wafting in. Its controller was council treasurer Harry Budd.

By the end of the month, the expectancy of war had reached fever pitch – and the number of ARP volunteers far exceeded the requested number.

The decent Nazi

A captain in the German air force travelled from Prague to Birmingham to give evidence at the assizes . . . for a Solihull man, who successfully claimed £5,029 1s damages for injury and loss through a collision with a car owned by an Erdington man.

He was Captain Arthur Jacobi, a fellow competitor of Wilberforce Noel Jordan, aged 31, of Wadleys Road, Solihull in the 1937 Six Days International Motor Cycle Trial, and he corroborated his evidence in the claim for damages.

Mr Jordan said that his right knee had been partly crippled in the accident in Watling Street in Penkridge, Staffordshire, on 17 July 1937.

(WCN, April 1939)

The sunny side of the street

"Absurd" and "unnecessary are the words most frequently applied to the government evacuation scheme as it concerns Solihull.

The district, a rapidly developing and in some cases a thickly-populated area on the doorstep of Birmingham, and in a direct line between this danger spot and another, Coventry, is included in those areas which the Ministry of Health considers suitable for the reception of children from large cities.

The ministry ordered ARP wardens to draw up a list of all houses suitable for taking evacuees. The Birmingham boundary was the line over which children had to be evacuated into Solihull.

But did that make them any safer?

Mrs Smith, of Lincoln Road, Olton, (where the boundary ran down the middle) said it would be silly to take her children to a house across the road and consider at the same time that they had reached a safe area.

Mr Duckett of Lincoln Road . . . pointed out that the Solihull side of the road was if anything less safe than the Birmingham side, because the railway line, a sure guide for aircraft, was nearer the Olton houses.

(WCN, January 1939)

Back on the road again

Banned driver William Kennedy, of Yoxall Road, Shirley, a caretaker at Sharmans Cross junior school, applied to the magistrates for his licence back with six months still to serve in 1939 – so he could become an Air Raid Precautions driver . . . but police objected, saying that they had heard nothing about his application before.

The bench held back the case while Sergeant Ashby accompanied Kennedy to the Solihull ARP office to determine if he had really applied.

His application form had indeed arrived that very morning, and so his request was granted – on condition he drove only ambulances.

After war was declared, many drivers facing motoring offences had the charges struck off on account of the national emergency.

The evil day comes . . .

Mr Chamberlain's broadcast on 3 September 1939 that Britain was at war was relayed to churghgoers at St Alphege.

The verger, Cliff Joiner, had a radio outside and told the rector, Rev Edward Fraser, who announced the grim yet inevitable news from the pulpit.

Members of the UDC heard the broadcast over a wireless in the council chamber as they sat for an emergency meeting.

Put that light out!

After war was declared, ARP wardens went to town with a vengeance on anyone found showing the slightest glimmer of light from a window, a car headlamp, or even a cigarette.

Warden Hodges of *Dad's Army* was no comic exaggeration.

Among the hordes of blackout breakers who replaced the endless stream of motorists at court was Lilian Lane of New Road, herself an ARP worker, went on duty and left four lights on at home – and was fined £2.

Gilbert Bayliss, of Glendale, Meriden Road, Hampton, said that a light in his house must have been left on by the maid.

After he was fined 10s, the clerk suggested he stopped 6d a week from her wages.

Amy Dyke, of Chamberlain Crescent, who was rude to officers who found a light had been showing for seven minutes, was fined 10s.

Her husband was told it would be heavier next time, particularly if his wife was abusive again.

Harold Williams, 68, of Broad Oaks Road, Solihull, who pleaded not guilty, described one allegedly malicious warden as "prancing around like a howling Dervish", before he was found guilty and fined £2.

Solihull Council itself was fined £5 after neighbour Vera Jones, of High Street, "shopped" the authority for showing a light from a window in November 1940,.

Tragedy befell 72-year-old retired electrician Charles Wall who had told by neighbours in Alderbrook Road how dark the blackout made the street in September 1939.

He went outside to see for himself . . . and was immediately knocked down and killed by a special constable's patrol car being driven without lights.

Sitting it out

Anderson shelters in back gardens and their Morrison counterparts for under the kitchen able were the order of the day for most Silhillians – bar one, a Smethwick firm's proprietor, who was certainly not short of a few quid.

> *Luxury is not usually thought of in connection with air-raid shelters, but in the case of a shelter built in the garden of Mr John Fallon's house, 12 St Bernard's Road, Olton, the two are synonymous.*
>
> *The shelter, which has been constructed beneath the lawn, is a fine example of what can be done to improve conditions of life below ground.*
>
> *It is constructed of 12-inch thick reinforced concrete specially treated to*

*prevent the seepage of moisture, and is 40 feet long by eight feet wide . . .
above the roof are layers of granite blocks, each a foot in depth, and
separated by layers of earth, also a foot in depth.*

*The shelter is air conditioned, warn air being supplied through marine
vents by means of a small motor . . . the air is drawn in from outside through
a steel tube standing 33 feet above ground, at a height above that normally
reached by persistent gases.*

*The interior . . . s finished in cream . . . an attractive system of tubular
lighting has been arranged . . . divans are placed along either wall covered
with gaily-coloured material . . . loose matting on the floor may be rolled
back to allow dancing on the polished oak floor . . . a few chairs, a card
table, radio, flowers and a framed picture of the King and Queen are included
in the furnishings . . .*

(WCN, November 1939)

By contrast, William Smith, aged 29, a sanitary engineer, of Mill Lane, was sentenced
to six months hard labour in October 1940 for stealing Anderson shelters from the homes
of Birmingham people "who did not desire to use them".

First in, first out

Solihull's first Labour councillor – indeed the first to be nominated by any political
party on the UDC – resigned his Olton seat in February 1940. A schoolmaster, Coun W
E Brown's services were needed elsewhere under the evacuation scheme.

War on the home front

*Appearing before Solihull magistrates because he had failed to pay £3 3s 6d
for his wife and child under a maintenance order, William Benjamin Elt, of
Stanway Road, Shirley, said that his wife had stripped his home.*

*His wife had taken all his furniture. "I was out for about an hour and a
half," he said "and when I came back she had taken everything. The house
was stripped and even my gas mask had gone".*

(WCN, March 1940)

A mixed reception

Solihull also became a reception area for evacuees from London's blitzed East End and
Coventry.

While many local people did their best to make their "guests" welcome, others still
regarded their home as their castle, and barred it accordingly . . .

*For failing to comply with the requirements of a billeting order in respect of
three Coventry evacuee children on November 19th, Horace Gladstone
Thompson, of Station Road, Knowle, was fined £5, with an alternative of
one month in prison, at Solihull Police court . . . the first case of its kind in
the district.*

Mr C Winterton, prosecuting for the Solihull Billeting Authority, said ...
there were nine habitable rooms in the defendant's home with five normal
residents ... owing to the serious bombing at Coventry, large numbers of
evacuees had arrived in the area ... but Mrs Thompson ... refused.

Later the same day two small boys and a little girl were taken to
defendant's home and Mrs Thompson ... allegedly replied: 'You can bring
them in if you like, but I shall put them out into the road'.

"The children cried a lot and felt that they were not wanted."
                                                                        (WCN December 1940)

Too much hospitality could also land you in court. Stanley Morris, of Windmill Lane, Dorridge, was summonsed for failing to report the arrival of an 'alien' at his home – Emma Kohn, a refugee firstly from Czechoslovakia and later from Coventry, one of several who Morris kindly suggested could stay with him.

In court Mrs Kohn emphasised the fact she was not a German but a full-blooded Czech ... and the charges were therefore dismissed.

Yet clashes between the needs of evacuees and their often-enforced hosts were by no means infrequent and were causing "considerable alarm", as Mr C Robinson, billing committee chairman, wrote in November 1941:

At least one evacuee was offered, by the householder, their fare to return home: in
another case the whole of the furniture including the carpet was removed from the room
the evacuees had to habit; in other cases the evacuees were made so uncomfortable in
one way or another that they preferred to leave ...

A group of Colliers Wood, London children who appeared before Solihull magistrates in October 1944 presented the other side of the coin.

Magistrate John Burman said the boys had "plundered the whole county", committing numerous burglaries and thefts, and generally being out of control. One was sent to approved school for two years.

One for the future

A new school which certainly met with approval was founded on 24 November 1941 by two women – Miss C Thirza Tucker and Miss Zelie G Bull.

The pair felt there was a need for a Church of England school in Solihull run on public school lines.

Named St Martin's, it opened at a house in Homer Road with just 14 girls ... and never looked back, becoming an independent public school in the early sixties.

Double standards?

Among the conscientious objectors who appeared before the Midland
Tribunal in Birmingham were several accountants ... whose firms included
munitions factories among their clients.

One of them, Henry Kite, of Burman Road, Shirley, said to be associated
with Wythall Baptist church, was told he was being treated very leniently
when he was ordered to do non-combatant service in the Army.

William Beevers, a trade union organiser, of Acheson Road, Shirley, intimated his intention to appeal when he was registered for non combatant work.

"If, under Hitler, you wouldn't read a single newspaper, go to a single church, have a single trade union, attend a trade union meeting, listen to a single wireless station, except what the Government said you could, what would you do then?" asked the judge.

"I should resist", said Beevers.

"That is what we are asking you to do," retorted the judge.

(WCN, December 1941)

Raids

Searchlight batteries were erected and barrage balloons littered Solihull skies in a bid to impede city-bound bombers, and the ARP service had the job of manning smokescreens, burning old rags and crude oil in barrels to obscure Nazi pilots' vision over potential targets like Cranmore industrial estate, where buildings were camouflaged with paint.

Solihull got off lightly when compared to its neighbours to the north and east, but there were still casualties and extensive damage to homes.

The first rescue took place in Barn Lane, Olton, when a bomb demolished one of a pair of semi-detached houses. Three people were brought out to safety after part of the dividing wall was removed.

A Coventry-bound German bomber was hit and dropped its deadly cargo over to lose weight – hitting a chemists shop, Duddy's wool shop, part of the White Cat cafe, while others fell in Malvern Park, in the worst town centre raid in mid-November 1940.

The most devastating raid, however, took place at 6.15am on 27 July 1942. A lone raider missed the Rover factory but emptied his cargo of bombs on to residential Alston Road.

Eleven people died, including a family of six named Pinder, and another 32 were injured, while a gaping crater lay in the space occupied by semi-detached council homes only seconds before.

Nearby Solihull Gas Works in Lode Lane was a regular target, although it was never hit. The Olton railway viaduct was a much sought-after target, but only once was part of the line blocked, and no trains were cancelled.

Shirley's BSA works was also targeted. A man watching one night time raid in a parked car by the George & Dragon pub was killed by flying shrapnel.

Wartime reporting restrictions led to a news blackout on individual incidents at the time, but figures published in September 1944 showed that the sirens sounded 358 warnings, and 49 actual raids with 517 incidents and "many thousands" of incendiary bombs.

The raids in the district, it was reported, had left 41 dead, 78 hospital cases, 196 minor injuries dealt with by First Aid Posts, 49 houses destroyed, 3,850 damaged, with 492 high explosive bombs, 24 delayed action bombs and one parachute mine dropped.

During wartime, the infirmary wards at the old workhouse had been given an new lease of life as an emergency hospital although its facilities were squalid and inadequate, and staffs like surgeon Paul Quinet furnished it with his own equipment.

A military auxiliary hospital appeared at Tudor Grange, kindly loaned by Lady Bird.

Soldiers at Fulford Hall Farm near Earlswood with the Heinkel III shot down on 11 May 1941.

The Air Training Corps gliding school at Knowle Hall was the first of its kind when opened in October 1942. This picture shows a glider being hitched to the back of a car ready for take off. (Britain DID win the war, it is stressed.)
Hockley Heath's wartime airfield at Box Trees which had been used for night flying training and a relief landing ground was also used as a gliding training school from June 1944.

Down and out in Earlswood

Three crew members of a German bomber were killed when it was brought down in a field Rumbush Lane on 11 May 1941, while a fourth survived his injuries. It was believed that the Heinkel III, the only plane to have been downed in Solihull, had been trying to find the Austin factory at Longbridge and may have lost its bearing.

A Home Guard Lewis gun was believed to have fired the few last shots which brought it down.

William Perry of Earlswood, a member of the Home Guard was later fined 40s by Solihull magistrates for failing to report finding a scorched pair of gloves belonging to one of the dead officers which he kept as a memento.

The three fatalities were interred at Robin Hood cemetery where young children regularly put flowers on their graves, and later reburied at the German war cemetery at Cannock Chase.

Still one of us

> A Home Office committee has decided that there is no foundation for an allegation against the Chief Constable of Warwickshire, Commander F R Kemble that the discipline of his force is created by fear or a discipline of the character exacted in a Gestapo system.
>
> (WCN, January 1942)

Food for all

Saturday 13 June saw the official opening of Solihull's British Restaurant by council leader H B Shaw in the former Mill Lane boys school.

The aim was to provide a restaurant where everyone and anyone could go for a meal at an affordable price. Catering for workman lacking a canteen and also school dinners, it accommodated up to 250 a time.

A typical lunch costing 1s 2d consisted of soup, beef, baked and boiled potatoes, cabbage, apple pie and custard.

A child's two-course midday meal cost 6d. Subsequent British Restaurants appeared in Stratford Road, Shirley, on the site of the present post office, (officially opened by the BBC's Freddie Grisewood) and finally Olton, in 1944, after a three-year delay.

A mother's Dunkirk

> 'I have a mother's heart, I couldn't send him back' said Eunice Tolman, aged 41, of Hurdis Road, Shirley, when she was at Solihull Police Court sent to prison for one month for harbouring her son, an Army deserter...
>
> A number officers went to her new address as a result of information received and surrounded the house.
>
> Eventually the deserter was found in civilian clothing, hiding behind a bedroom door...

'My son has done his bit,' said the defendant. 'He came back from Dunkirk with his nerves shattered, and I couldn't give him up."

(WCN, June 1942)

Who do you think you are kidding, Mr Hitler?

For unlawfully absenting himself from Home Guard duty without reasonable excuse on 23 August, 26 and 28, David Norton, of Balsall Street, Balsall Common, was ordered to pay fines and costs totally £10 5s by the Solihull magistrates . . . an alternative of 14 days imprisonment . . . was fixed.

Norton had said (in a letter) that the only reason for not attending parades was the lack of petrol . . . and since the basic allowance of petrol had been discontinued, he had no means of transport.

Witness said that defendant's home was about ten minutes walk from his place of duty.

(WCN, October 1942)

And complaints were received from allotment holders in Malvern Park – one of many public open spaces adapted from growing essential foodstuffs – about damage caused by cattle straying from an adjacent far. But:

Upon investigation, it was found that the real culprits were the Home Guard who, during their exercise, had cut and pulled down barbed wire across a brook . . .

After discussions between the farmer and council officials, it was decided to erect

Solihull's Home Guard stage a victory parade along Poplar Road outside the Council House.

hurdles across the brook, so that the unwelcome visitors will be unable to make further inroads on growing crops.

Solihull's Home Guard platoon, which started life in 1939 as the Local Defence Volunteers, armed with pikes and pitchforks, had its headquarters in Touchwood Hall. While its early efforts received thanks in "in jeers, in derision and in doubts," because they were "inept, ill armed and ill equipped", the platoon had made themselves in three years "a superb fighting force", it was reported in May 1943, and several thousand people turned out to cheer them at a town centre parade.

However, that was not the final word . . .

> *During a recent big scale Home Guard exercise in which American troops took part, a detachment of enthusiastic Home Guards men marched into Solihull police station with a request for 'formal surrender', the station having been declared a 'capture'.*
>
> *The bewilderment of the local constabulary, who were unaware alike of the existence of the exercise and that their home from home was regarded as an objective, was understandable.*
>
> *It was learned that Solihull was, in fact, outside the zone of operations and that the Home Guard, like Alexander, looking for fresh fields to conquer, had with a superabundance of zeal, unwittingly wandered out of the area in which they had been allotted.*
>
> (WCN, March 1944)

Waste not want not

> *Over 11 tons of waste paper and more than 1,000lb of rubber have been collected by schools of the urban district this term.*
>
> *Solihull schoolchildren . . . will be thrilled to know that in providing rubber for 160 dinghies they have been instrumental in saving the lives of 160 airmen.*
>
> *Cedarhurst School with 400lb of rubber to its credit, is one of the most successful scavengers, followed closely by Knowle Church of England School, Malvern Hall and Lode Heath.*
>
> *At least one Solihull family has a "Victory" bowl into which each tiny scrap of paper is placed. This is confidently expected to yield a rich haul during the Christmas holidays – present wrappings, toffee papers and even mottoes out of crackers.*
>
> (WCN, December 1942)

By April 1944, the total amount of salvage collected in Solihull amounted to more than 4,000 tons, and was worth £26,000.

Wastage of petrol was a criminal offence. To deviate from an authorised route from home to work could land you in the dock.

'You want young men of your own age to sacrifice their lives so that you can ride in comfort to your work. Why don't you use a bicycle?' asked Mr Wild, clerk of the justices at Solihull Police court when Edwin Pearce, of Hay Tor, Trueman's Heath, was summoned for using petrol unlawfully.

Pearce's misdemeanour was that he had gone three-and-a-half miles out of his way home to visit his sister in Knowle, and was fined 20s.

Bonds of friendship

Solihull adopted its own V/W class destroyer, HMS Vivacious, in 1942, with civic dignitaries and ships officers exchanging commemorative plaques. An HMS Vivacious Comforts Fund was established.

It is intended to invite members of the ship's company to Solihull whenever the ship is in port to arrange accommodation for them, and to provide entertainment for them while they are here . . .

In March 1944, around 100 HMS Vivacious crewmen visited Solihull, enjoying a civic reception, a dance in the Council House Assembly Hall complete with can-can girls and a slap-up meal at the British Restaurant. They also played a soccer match against local Nalgo officials.

Five Churchill tanks were named after areas of the urban district after a "Tanks For Attack" campaign in 1942.

Solihull people had also been quick to dip into their pockets for events like War Weapons Week, when a "gratifying" £150,000 was raised in October 1940, and Warship Week the following March, with "well over" half a million pounds raised.

One anonymous woman turned up at the Council House and dropped a folded piece of paper containing 10s simply signed "from a sailor's mother" and walked off . . .

Changed allegiances during the global conflict saw Solihull's first "twinning" link established in 1943 . . . with a Russian town! Maikop, in the Caucasians, had recently been liberated by the Soviets when the tide turned against the Nazi invasion on the eastern front.

The red flag flew over Solihull on many occasions, with proceeds from street collections devoted to the rehabilitation of Red Army wounded, and a British-Soviet unity committee having a flourishing local branch.

The conversion of Italy from an Axis to an Allied power brought a change in conditions for POWs from there. Much resentment was expressed by bombed-out Bristolian Arthur Aston who was living in a garage in Dickens Heath with his wife and four children.

He complained that Italian ex-prisoners were being found accommodation in first-class hotels and farms and taken to work in luxury coaches.

"And we never saw a banana for six years"

> *A concert organised under the auspices of the Solihull Police Victory Garden Show committee at the Midland Counties Institution, Knowle . . . £70 was raised for Red Cross funds.*
>
> *A number of gifts added considerably to the funds. A lemon, for instance, was bought and given back for resale three times and raised a total of £5 2s.*
>
> (WCN, March 1943)

While ration books were the order of the day, there would always be those looking for that little extra . . . and those who would be prepared to provide it:

> *A police officer who, at the request of a woman friend, bought a goose for her bedridden husband's dinner, charged her more than double what it had*

cost and accepted an "extra sum" for his trouble, was brought before Solihull magistrates, charged with buying and selling the bird at a price above the maximum controlled price and with making a false declaration.

Mr C C Ladds, prosecuting, said that a painful feature of the case was that the defendant (PC Andrew Stonehouse, based at Shirley) was one whose duty it was to see that the public did not infringe the very regulations he himself had broken.

(WCN, March 1943)

A wannabe

Reports of the bravery of the multitude of Solihull men in active service in the various corners of the globe were legion, and they would easily require a separate book to even begin to deal with them. The reporting of their exploits became more frequent as censorship relaxed in the latter days.

It was inevitable that their Boys Own flavour would inspire many a youngster . . . . . .

Roger Stanley Hemming, 15, only son of Mr & Mrs Hemming of Hampton Lane, Solihull, had a longing to join the Merchant Navy.

A studious boy, he had, with the aid of compasses, worked out a route and with £11 in his pocket . . . he set off for the Welsh coast on his bicycle intending to cross from there to Ireland on a rowing boat.

At Aberystwyth, he abandoned his bicycle and hid some of his money under a hayrick . . . he slept each night in a hut on the beach, waiting for his chance.

As he came out of a picture house, Roger was asked his name by a police officer . . . he still wore his school blazer and cap and was easily recognised . . .

There was, however, a happy ending for Roger:

Arrangements are being made to enter him at a naval college so that he can realise his ambition and go to sea.

Holidays At Home

Midland families were urged to save resources by taking holidays at home during the summer of 1943.

Solihull boasted a host of attractions, from the Great Dominion Circus in Olton Park to cabaret at Chapel Fields School and dancing on the green in Malvern Park.

No visitor to Solihull could have failed to realise that something was afoot on Saturday afternoon.

Each bus and tram came in loaded to capacity and the demeanour of the crowds which drifted along the High Street towards the Rover Sports at Malvern Park made it clear that the holiday spirit was abroad.

Horace's wartime gift

News of the most munificent gift ever made to the people of Solihull was disclosed . . . when the chairman of the council, (Coun James Harold Malley) announced that Mr Horace J Brueton had offered his house, together with 29 acres of grounds, for an all-time open space.

In a letter to the council, Mr Brueton writes: "We are favoured to live in one of the most attractive areas in the Midlands. The district was developed very quickly before the war and will no doubt continue do so afterwards . . .

"I am anxious to do my share in the postwar arrangements for the urban district by providing for all time an open space for the people to use – and which the council may preserve in all its present beauty . . . a very fine opportunity of linking up Malvern Park . . . to give the public an open space . . . from Solihull church to Sandalls Bridge . . ."

(WCN, January 1944)

The pool in Brueton Park had been used for ice skating in winter for generations – a pastime that was once guaranteed to empty all the town pubs in the bitterest of frosts.

Formally opened by Mr Burman in April 1944, the park would now be open all the year round forever.

Quality of life was also enhanced when Solihull Society of Arts was also formed in that year following a meeting called by Lady Bird and Dr Worrall.

The musical section's first event was a concert featuring Isabel Baillie and Michael Mullinar held in September.

The turning point

The United States forces set up their local headquarters in Blossomfield Road, on the site occupied by the Tudor Grange swimming baths.

Their canteen was in the Methodist church at the junction with Streetsbrook Road and local ladies delighted in serving them.

Officers were billeted with local families and their never-ending supply of sweets and souvenirs made them an instant hit with local children. The US Army medical corps were based at Knowle.

It was apparent that something big was in the air when the Americans drove south in convoys through Solihull and Knowle at the beginning of June 1944, never to return.

D-Day had arrived.

Knowle's tragic family

Mr and Mrs Young and family of Copt Heath Avenue, Knowle, have received word of the death in action of their son Dennis Young in Normandy on June 12.

This is the second son Mr and Mrs Young have lost during the war. They have two other sons still serving in the forces. In the last war, four out of five of Mrs Young's brothers were killed, and Mr Young himself was wounded . . .

(WCN, July 1944)

Dismiss!

The 5th Battalion of the Home Guard has gone cheerfully into retirement, cheerfully, that is, to the outward eye, but one felt that the stand down parade

> *at Solihull . . . was a face behind which many a man hid his feelings of pain*
> *in the parting of the ways . . . a swelling of 'Dear Old Pals, Jolly Old Pals'*
> *gave expression to an emotion which, despite their rough jocularity, one felt*
> *was astir in the hearts of these men.*
>
> (WCN, December 1944)

Figures showed that 6,595 men had been recruited under the leadership of Lt Col Frank Blennerhasset, with 1,177 going on to the forces or other Home Guard units. Capt Bernard Peace, founder member of the Shirley section, remembered the 5th battalion as one of the finest in the country at the finish.

Other services like the ARP were also largely stood down as the imminent collapse of Germany following the Allied liberation of western Europe made them no longer necessary.

Solihull's first MP

As the war years drew to a close, a major reorganisation of Parliamentary boundaries saw the old Tamworth division split up and new seats to cater for the growing towns of Sutton Coldfield and Solihull created.

Solihull's first Tory candidate was distinguished army officer and adventurer Sir Martin Lindsay, aged 40, who in 1934 had led the world's longest-ever self supporting sledge journey across Greenland, and who was to have stood for Brigg & Scunthorpe until the outbreak of war suspended the forthcoming General Election.

His opponent was a young Royal Artillery captain who was wounded at Dunkirk – Roy Jenkins – who later represented Stechford at 27 years, became one of the youngest-ever Labour Home Secretaries and later split to form the Social Democrats as one of the "Gang of Four". Although 1945 saw a Labour landslide, Sir Martin won by 26,696 votes to 21,647, with a little help from Winston Churchill, who addressed crowds outside the Conservative committee room in Warwick Road during a fleeting visit on June 25.

The gentle touch

> *Two attractive young women made local history this week. They are APW*
> *Cope and APW Beal – the first women patrol officers to walk a beat in the*
> *Solihull Police Division.*
>
> *Both attached to Shirley, their appointment followed the serious depletion*
> *of the police force in that area (due to conscription) . . .*
>
> (WCN, February 1945)

Peace at last!

> *In Solihull, VE Day coincided with a civic dinner, and official arrangements*
> *had been confined to the parks, where bonfires and dancing on the green*
> *(with fireworks privately provided from goodness knows what carefully-*
> *hoarded store) attracted crowds until the early hours and passed off without*
> *incident, save for what might have been a serious accident when a young*
> *woman's hair was set alight by a carelessly thrown rocket.*

There were two centres of attraction in the village – the Brueton Gardens, bathed in a delightful golden glow, and the floodlit church. At midnight the streets were still thronged.

There was an atmosphere of quiet contentment, but little indication of an excess of spirits in either sense) and the calm was shattered only by sporadic bursts of song and the shrill squeals of excited children. "Much quieter than we expected and certainly much quieter than after the last war," was the verdict of the police.

The large illuminated V-sign on the Council House brought passers-by to a standstill . . .

(WCN, May 1945)

Street parties were the order of the day throughout the district on that day in May 1945, with Hitler's effigy being burned from a lamp post in Redlands Road – a similar fate awaiting figures of Japanese commanders when similar celebrations were held for VJ Day in August.

VJ Party, Ulleries Road, 15 August 1945, when families gathered together to mark he first real day of peace. Children's sports in Olton Park were followed by a tea party in which resident Ernest Jones, the boss of Digbeth printers H & E Jones Ltd., presented all the youngsters with books.
In the evening the adults enjoyed games, dancing, and a bonfire with fireworks. Local resident and partygoer Mrs Gwenyth Arnold (nee Jones) then just 11, said: "To me the war was the bombs dropping in the fields behind the houses which are now Lyndon School playing fields, the blackouts, the funny glass in the window and collecting the shrapnel."

THE NEWS. SATURDAY, 29 APRIL, 1944

GO INTO ACTION · with *your Savings*

To him, the British Soldier, 'going into action'
means danger . . . mine-strewn wastes . . . clutch-
ing coils of tangled wire . . . shells . . . mud
. . . lack of sleep. But he never falters. And
we ? . All we are asked as we 'go into action'
during SALUTE THE SOLDIER WEEK—is to spend
less . . . to go without those things we do not
need, and to save . . . to break all records with
our savings.

SALUTE THE SOLDIER WEEK

INVEST ALL YOU CAN IN —
3% *Savings Bonds 1960-70* · 3¼% *National War
Bonds 1952-54* · 3% *Defence Bonds* · *Savings Certificates* · *Savings
Stamps* · *The Post Office Savings Bank* · *Birmingham Municipal Bank*

'What is peacetime like?'

He has grown up in the biggest war of all
time. He hasn't known what peace meant.
it is going to be a strange and wonderful
new world.
Whatever happiness ' after the war ' has in
store for him, one thing will count most —
good health.
During wartime you have found how 'Milk
of Magnesia ' has helped to keep him fit and
free from minor stomach troubles.
In the happier days ahead, ' Milk- of
Magnesia ' will, even as now- be your stand-
by — never absent 'from the medicine
cabinet.

'MILK OF MAGNESIA'

Chapter Six

A TIDAL WAVE OF PROGRESS
1945–59

Major postwar expansion was on the agenda in Solihull well before the end of hostilities was in sight.

The district council agreed in March 1943 to increase the rate by 1s 7d in the pound to enable it to make strategic land purchases.

The 113-acre Elmdon Hall estate was bought as public open space, but councillors decided not to acquire empty the 600-year-old Manor House in Solihull High Street.

The former dower house of Solihull's Greswolde family was being advertised in 1944 as being "of particular interest to cinema proprietors, chain stores and multiple shop companies", in other words, demolition.

Overtures were made by conservationists and the owners agreed to hold off until March 1945, when a local fundraising campaign to buy the half-timbered house for public use proved successful at the eleventh hour.

While this particular landmark was saved, the changes that the postwar world was bringing made it clear that drastic changes would have to be made elsewhere in the town centre.

The easing of petrol restrictions back to the basic ration, for instance, added thousands of private cars to military and commercial traffic, and by November 1945, a bypass, one-way system, parking restrictions and other traffic-calming measures for the shopping area were being proposed.

On a far larger scale, schemes for a new trunk road scheme crossing the West Midlands conurbation from the Humber estuary and linking it to South Wales via a Severn Bridge were under serious discussion, and its route through Solihull was not wholly unlike that taken by the M42 three decades later. Fears were expressed that the "autobahn" would split the district in two.

The UDC vowed regardless to maintain the balance between Solihull's rural heritage and the fresh demands heaped on it:

> Determined to preserve the pleasant residential character of Solihull, but to allow it to develop as a self-contained community, independent of Birmingham, Solihull Council approved a long-term plan, submitted by the Surveyor, Mr C R Hutchinson.
>
> The plans shows the district surrounded by a green belt, with a central "core" developed on neighbourhood unit lines and indicates village development in outlying areas.
>
> (WCN, October 1946)

Another world war had, however, left homelessness in abundance in its wake, and Solihull launched a new type of temporary prefabricated bungalow in Highwood Avenue in a bid to reduce the UDC's 2,000-strong growing waiting list.

One of the first tenants, Mrs E Jones from Dorridge, said she was "absolutely delighted", although much consternation was expressed by others at the weekly rent of 17s 9d compared to 13s for city prefabs.

Elsewhere, makeshift homes mushroomed again with the former RAF airfield at Hockley Heath becoming home to 20 squatters in huts and caravan dwellers flocking into the rural areas.

Squatters backed by the Birmingham Communist Party took matters into their own hands when they occupied the 16-room former ARP headquarters at The Grove in Lode Lane to escape cramped conditions elsewhere and six-year housing waiting lists in Birmingham, but eventually agreed to go quietly.

Homes for workers at Solihull's new breed of factories were desperately needed.

The Rover company protested when the Ideal Benefit Society was authorised to erect 300 houses – then had its licence withdrawn after only 47 were built, while the company was having to bus in 500 workers daily from its Coventry headquarters. In Shirley, a new council estate covered meadows around Cranmore Boulevard adjacent to the Highlands Road factories.

Despite Solihull's alluring image of affluence and desirability, nearly 700 Solihull homes still lacked a sewage connection in 1950, and relied on dumbwells.

In 1950 the council earmarked farmland at Hobs Moat for the district's first "town within a town", giving planners a 100-acre virgin site between Coventry Road, Hobs Moat Road and Lyndon Road to design an "ideal neighbourhood" from scratch, with both private and municipal homes.

Lode Lane, once described as the loveliest road in Warwickshire, lost its delightful rural character forever, while the new £20,000 Lyndon Methodist church opened to serve the new district in 1959.

Elsewhere, more housing estates surged into the rural fringe.

Olton's medieval Chapel Fields Farm went to the bulldozer despite a campaign to save it; the watermeadows between Streetsbrook Road and Prospect Lane along with Monks Farm vanished; the 300-year-old windmill in Solihull Lodge was gelignited in 1957 to make way for an extra house in Coton Grove.

In the town centre, Victorian Sutton Lodge was replaced by a new parade of 20 shops with maisonettes above.

In a move predating the Thatcher Government's popular Right To Buy policy of the 1980s, tenants of UDC council houses were in 1952 sent a circular asking if, under certain approved conditions, they would wish to purchase them.

Enterprising would-be homeowners in Shirley followed a different course – and built the own bungalows for £1,150 each. The 50-member Solihull Progressive Housing Association trained for nine months before starting work on their own estate in Dovedale Avenue in 1952.

By 1956, Solihull had the sixth best record in the country for postwar housebuilding, with nearly 6,000 having been completed since April 1945.

The Royal Oak Hotel in 1948. It stood at the junction of Drury Lane and High Street until it was demolished to make way for the town centre redevelopment scheme

One of 50 lucky Silhillians receives a monster food parcel from UDC chairman Coun Maurice Walker at the corner of Lode Lane and Grove Road in July 1949. A consignment was donated by well-wishers in the United States through C.A.R.E (Co-operative for American Remittances to Europe). The war may have ended four years before, but local suffering and need caused by it had not.

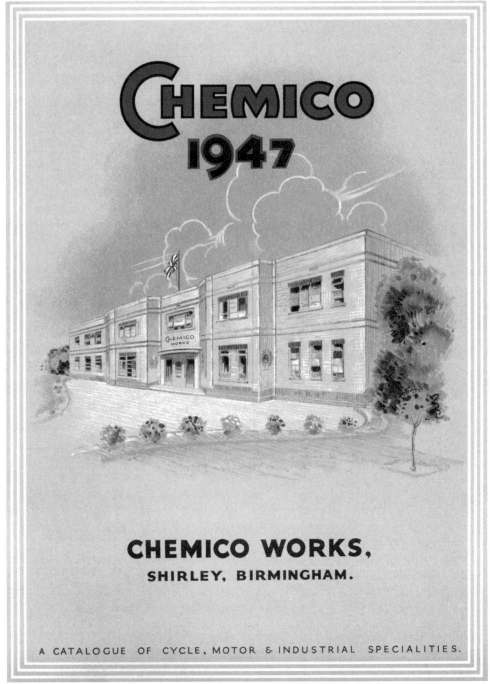

Chemico – the County Chemical Co Ltd – moved to this showpiece factory in Stratford Road, Shirley, in 1941.
The firm's distinctive pink Household Cleanser was exported to 64 countries and in 1915 it manufactured
the first gas bomb used by the Allies. Its most famous product – a mixture of brilliantine and cream – was
invented by employee Lambert G Hambreks in 1929. From Handsworth Wood to Hollywood, Brylcreem took
the world by storm.
Chemico is now based in Highlands Road, Shirley, the Stratford Road site having been redeveloped as a
Sainsbury supermarket.

The squeeze resumes

The war may have ended, but townsfolk were under no illusions that austerity had not. Therefore:

> *It was a pleasant surprise for Solihull people to find lemons on sale in the*
> *village shops on Shrove Tuesday. For what are pancakes without lemons?*
> (WCN, March 1946)

Townsfolk readily welcomed help from overseas. In October 1946, nearly 450 of Solihull's oldest residents received 56 cases of foodstuffs from people in Australia, each getting five tins of meat, two tins of marmalade, three bars of soap and a packet of dried apricots.

Mrs Frost, aged 86, from Damson Lane, who joined the lengthy foodqueue in the Council House, defied doctors orders to walk home with 14lbs of items.

The public at large were weary of going without in perpetuity, and August 1946 saw a massive rush for the seaside in the biggest exodus of holidaymakers since 1939. All 75 Midland Red long-distance coaches were booked up a month in advance and traffic on the Stratford Road in Shirley hit record levels.

Nevertheless, rationing still continued into the 1950s. Within hours of meat rationing ending in July 1954, Solihull butcher J T Tustin, whose modern slaughterhouse in Warwick Road had seen only four years work before the war broke out, was busy again, preparing 20 lambs from Eastcote Farm so his customers could once again enjoy "home killed" meat after so long.

A centre for educational excellence

Experts predicted that Solihull's population would rise to more than 100,000, and extra schools would be needed to serve the new estates.

As schemes were laid for four new grammar schools and two technical schools, the days of the old elementary schools seemed a world away. Not all, however, welcomed the large-scale changes: in June 1947 there were mixed feelings in Hockley Heath over plans to send the over 11s from the village's County Mixed and Infants School to a secondary school for the first time.

Warwickshire County Council acquired the huge Tudor Grange estate from the Bird family and planned to develop it as an educational centre. In addition to four new state schools and one run by the Roman Catholic church, there would also be a £3million technical college, upon which work started in 1958, four years after the first classes started in nearby Sutton Lodge in Blossomfield Road.

An indoor swimming pool and running track were to be built near Solihull railway station, adjoining the new 68-acre Tudor Grange Park, where a miniature golf course opened in 1957.

In 1959, 12 young Solihull men pushed a bed all the way to London's Pinewood Studios to boost publicity for the mayor's appeal to finance the £35,000 track and adjacent youth headquarters.

The first of these educational establishments, Tudor Grange Boys Grammar School, was opened amidst a blaze of publicity in September 1956, when a dedication service

A scene never to be repeated . . . a pleasant afternoon on Twinderrow's Pool, a popular but unofficial bathing haunt behind Cranmore Farm in Shirley, long since covered by an electricity substation and the ugly but functional buildings of Cranmore Industrial Estate.
It was here in 1948 that 14-year-old Reginald Gardiner of Cranmore Boulevard saved the life of Hazel Findon, 14, who had fallen in but could not swim.

The ultimate d-i-y enthusiasts of Solihull Progressive Housing Association build their own homes in Dovedale Avenue, Shirley, during 1952–54.

A red-letter day for these schoolboy trainspotters at Solihull station in August 1953. They are witnessing the rare arrival of a pioneering three-car diesel railbus produced by ACV Sales Ltd. The prototype gave an uncomfortable ride and other types of diesel multiple unit were instead adopted by British Rail, but the writing was already on the wall for steam traction.

Solihull councillors meet to decide the fate of the derelict Shirley Racecourse, which was redeveloped as Shirley Golf Club. The club was set up by a group of Jewish golfers who found themselves refused membership elsewhere, and bought the racecourse in 1955 for £19,500 on behalf of the Birmingham Jewish community.

headed by mayor Coun Hubert Moren-Brown was held at St Alphege church. Head-master Arthur Munday told his 450 boys that their ambition must be to make it the finest grammar school in the country. The corresponding girls' school opened for the 1959 summer term.

Washing up before class

> *For some years girls of Malvern Hall School have been doing the washing up after school meals because domestic help has not been available.*
> *Parents have felt strongly that this duty should be no part of school life and so, to render it unnecessary, the School Parents Association has offered to give the school a dishwashing machine . . .*
>
> (WCN, December 1947)

Heartbreak for a Shirley farmer

Reginald Cresswell was brought from America to Shirley by his parents as a sick young boy, who needed a life in the open air if he was to survive.

His parents bought Bronte Farm off Union Road so that he could enjoy a healthy life to an old age, which he did.

At the age of 75, Mr Cresswell was shocked to receive a demand from Solihull Council for his land – which was needed for the building of Shirley Heath County Primary School.

Mr Cresswell said quite categorically that not want to part with any of his land. "Since he has lived there, others have reaped a rich reward from the sale of property which has been needed for public purposes, but his only desire has been to end his days on the land where he has lived so long", pleaded Coun John Woollaston on his behalf.

But education chairman Coun Harry Miller replied that no other suitable site was available, as church halls, the former British Restaurant and a community centre were being used as makeshift classrooms for Shirley's youngsters.

Across the district, the number of primary school classes with up to 55 children had trebled within a year.

Mr Cresswell lost his appeal against a compulsory purchase order despite vociferous support from local people and work began in March 1952.

Scant consolation must have been the fact that one of the four "houses" of the school would be named Cresswell in his memory, along with Cooper, Miller and Newey.

Two secondary schools, Light Hall boys and girls, were earmarked for the western side of Shirley, on similar lines to Lyndon School but on more "austere" lines with less frills.

Knowle's Arden High School, Sharmans Cross Boys Modern School, Valley, Blossomfield, Greswolde and Streetsbrook infants schools were among others built in the 1950s to serve a population greatly boosted by the postwar baby boom . . .

Although grammar schools like Tudor Grange grabbed centre stage, the secondary modern schools were producing quite remarkable results, it was said. Sharmans Cross was attended by boys who had failed the 11-plus, some of who were astonishing everyone by getting several General Certificate of Education passes . . . a fact that made many in Solihull question the ethics of selective education.

Youth clasped by a woman

Warwick County Education Committee's proposal to put a six-foot group and statue – to cost £550 of public money – in the entrance hall of the new Lyndon Secondary School at Solihull raised a storm at this week's meeting of the Solihull education committee.

Entitled the Young Prometheus, the modernistic group shows the naked figure of an adolescent youth clasped by a woman, and symbolises, says the artist, Maurice Lambert, youth's acceptance of the restraining influence of authority, from which, at the same time, he struggles to free himself.

Members of the Solihull committee laughed as they gathered round to inspect photographs of the statuary. "Grotesque", "ridiculous" and "most unsuitable" were some of the comments.

(Solihull &Warwick County News, July 1950)

Coun James Harold Malley later raised misgivings about certain men shortlisted as governors for Lyndon School because of potential communist representation.

"Why should we have these people taking part in our local government when nationally they are being expelled from government positions?", he asked.

A blackboard jungle?

The importation into the school of a man-eating tiger would be no less dangerous.

So said expert carpenter Coun Rev J A E Jones, at a meeting of Solihull's education committee in May 1950, when Sharmans Cross Secondary Modern School governors asked for a grant to install a large electrical circular saw – given by the Parents Association – in the handicraft room.

Medical pioneers

Eight brothers and sisters, all the chidden of Mrs Dorothy Brown, of Marshall Lake Road, Shirley, were the first youngsters to benefit from ultra-violet ray treatment, a new service, started . . . at the Shirley Infant Welfare Centre held at the Institute, School Road.

Although the benefits of the ray are almost equal to those of a holiday by the sea, the participants did not all co-operate without some protest.

There were tearful and bewildered faces, and some of the tiniest obviously disapproved of their sun goggles, trying to pull them off the moment mother's back was turned.

(WCN, January 1948)

Solihull also had its first visits of the Mass Radiography Unit, at Shirley Institute in June 1948 and the Manor House the following month, where free X-ray examinations would screen the ordinary man in the street for the dreaded tuberculosis.

A 40-year-old Irishman, Dr Ian McLachlan, was appointed Solihull's first medical officer of health.

In 1952 he found that out of a child population of 11,000, there were 9,000 who had not seen a dentist within 12 months, while the others had been in pain before treatment was given. And a survey of 3,261 pupils in 1953 found that 1,869 had medical 'defects'.

Conditions at Solihull Hospital – which had evolved in the old workhouse infirmary during the war – were slated by Solihull Residents Association, which claimed that ill people could not be sure of a bed there. Members called for a new hospital to be built.

Coun Bill Wright of the Friends of Solihull Hospital Association stated that hospitals in the colonies were "ten times better" and called for cash to be spent on health rather than education.

Better communications

> With the extension of the "999" scheme to the Knowle and Dorridge telephone area, local residents are now able to obtain priority emergency calls.
>
> The scheme has been operating in Solihull for the past 12 months. It enables a caller, by dialling 999 instead of 0, to secure the special attention of the operator for calls to the fire, police or ambulance service on occasions of emergency . . .

(WCN, January 1948)

Silhill Hall – the prominent local landmark sketched by prominent local surgeon Paul Quinet – before its untimely and outrageous destruction in the sixties.

The desire in some quarters to obtain for Solihull its own postal area, separate from Birmingham, is not "snobbery", but one expression of local patriotism . . . any Silhillian with a pride in his borough would desire that it stood alone.

(Solihull News, January 1954)

"Solihull, Warwickshire" began on 29 January 1956.

Solihull's worldbeater is born

Some 20 Midland pressmen visited the Rover company's works at Solihull and were introduced to an entirely new product – "The Land Rover".

Designed primarily as a "maid of all work" for the farmer, the countryman and for general industrial use, it will make its first public appearance at the Amsterdam Motor Show on April 30th.

"I saw it undergoing tests of the severest kind, and it is a great-hearted little machine," writes a News reporter.

Mr A B Wilks, managing director of the company, said that much of the practical testing had been done on a Solihull farm and the results had been eminently satisfactory.

(WCN, April 1948)

Ve haf ways of making you buy . . . in a Cold War scene from 1957, West German Land Rover dealers visit the Lode Lane plant to inspect the standard model of which more than 500 supplied to frontier guards along the Iron Curtain.
The 1,000,000th Land Rover was driven off the track in 1975.

Worldwide interest focused on the Lode Lane factory again in 1950 when Rover announced it had produced the first gas-turbine car, one which would reach speeds of more than 150mph.

The company became so successful, with export orders totalling £70million in its first decade, and a test track two-and-a-half-miles long, the only one of its kind in Britain, was built at Lode Lane.

The valve wireless has had its day

> *A small group of Chadwick End people, including Father Dale, "looked in" on the Buckingham Palace and St Paul's Silver Wedding scenes . . . weather conditions . . . were ideal for television reception and though a standard London set was being used at a point 80 miles or more beyond the normal range of the Alexandra Park station, then pictures were good, some of them in fact excellent . . .*
>
> (WCN, May 1945)

The Sutton Coldfield transmitter station opened in 1949 and brought clear reception to six million people living within a 50-mile radius.

The new-fangled medium did not find favour with all. In 1954, Rev Lionel Bailey, vicar of St Phillip's, Dorridge, preached against the broadcasting of a circus during Sunday services. He was even against televising church services themselves.

Urbs in Rure

Solihull's coat of arms was unveiled in July 1948.

Three historic families, the Throckmortons, the Odingsells and the Greswoldes were represented by two bars, two stars and a greyhound respectively, a crown symbolised the town's Saxon connections and an oak tree alluded to the old Forest of Arden.

A walled tower and two sickles indicated that while the district contained large residential areas, much of it was still mainly agricultural.

The motto, *Urbs in Rure*, spoke for itself.

A nuclear strike in Solihull

A spectacular "atomic bomb" explosion filled the Assembly Hall of Solihull's Council House on Monday night, and left the people who attended the Civil Defence recruiting meeting with plenty of food for thought.

In the centre of the hall a table-top model of Hiroshima was "bombed" by a model plane. Standing well back, spectators felt the heat of the explosion on their faces as a lurid column of fire curled four or five feet into the air . . .

Council chairman Maurice Walker deplored the poor response to a campaign to attract more Civil Defence volunteers at the Cold Way plummeted well below sub zero.

While the population had reached nearly 70,000, only 20 had applied, despite popular forebodings of war against the Soviet Union.

County Civil Defence officer Lt Col F F C Watkins had harsher words to say at the meeting in April 1950:

People who rush into print and declare that five to ten atom bombs on this country would finish us are lunatics of the first order and should be locked up as a menace to the public morale . . ."

The ordinary Anderson shelter with two-and-a-half feet of concrete was proof against atomic blast, heat and radiation, providing it was outside the 100 per cent circle of damage, he said.

The Civil Defence organisation established new headquarters in outbuildings at Sutton Lodge in 1952.

The first of many

One man's conscience has caused a complete standstill at the Rover company's works.

Because 33-year-old Irishman James McElroy of Elmdon Park Road joined the Plymouth Brethren – a religious sect which forbids trade union membership – and resigned from the National Union of Vehicle Builders, the staff of the car body assembly shop where McElroy works, refused . . . to work with him, now he is no longer a union man.

They demanded that he be dismissed or compelled to rejoin the union, so that the "closed shop" which they say exists in the department is maintained.

By Thursday night, the entire staff of the shop – some 700 workers – were on strike. And . . . after a morning meeting of strikers had voted solidly in favour of a general stoppage, nearly 3,000 in all downed tools . . .

(Solihull & Warwick County News, August 1950)

Children in the dock

"In my day and age the local policeman who caught youngsters in the act meted out his own justice – a short sharp smack across the head – and if the boy complained to his parents, he would get another . . ."

But is this often-expressed nostalgia by the older generation about the punishment of juvenile crime in former days justified? A glance at court reports from the early fifties shows that children often appeared before the bench for comparatively trivial matters.

"We are really concerned with these offences, and are afraid serious accidents may result from them", said Inspector H W Randle at Solihull juvenile court when a 10-year-old boy admitted riding past a "halt" sign on his bicycle without stopping, and was fined 5s.

"They want whipping. If they come here again I only hope I am here to deal with them," said chairman of the bench Coun Miller, after fining five boys aged 14–16 for damaging hayricks on a farm sums ranging from 5s to £2 10s.

Two boys aged 12 and 14 who went camping at Knowle and stole eggs from a poultry farmer for their breakfast, along with a pair of Wellington boots, appeared. One was sent to an approved school and the other given 12 months probation.

Fines of 7s 6d each were imposed on two teenage boys who played "cycle tag" on the pavement in Ulverley Green Road.

In 1959, the Rector of Elmdon and Bickenhill, the Rev Jack Reed, angered by persistent vandalism at his church and school premises, called for the reintroduction of physical punishment: *"Juvenile courts should have the power to administer the cane, followed by an introduction to Christianity so they can be taught a better attitude to life"*.

What would he have made of nineties Britain, with Safari Boy being taken on an African dream holiday to "cure" his villainy and social workers paying Pocket Money Boy a weekly allowance not to commit crime?

A motorbike made for two

A Shirley man and his girlfriend were both driving the same motorcycle along a country lane near Earlswood when their machine was involved in an accident after passing a "halt" sign without stopping, Henley-in-Arden magistrates were told.

The case was described as being very unusual as both riders of the motorcycle were accused of the same offence at the same time.

Pipefitter Jack Abrahall, 24, of Tanworth Lane, Shirley, and Joy Coldicott, 17, of Cranmore Road, Shirley, were both found guilty of driving without due care and attention and were fined £4 and 30s respectively, both with 12-month bans.

Chief Inspector R Wardman said the young lady was sitting in the saddle holding the handlebars and manipulating the gears while her friend was sitting on the pillion seat working the clutch and throttle.

The greatest day of all

Solihull was one of the first Midland authorities to send a telegram of sympathy to the Queen Mother Death of King George VI on 6 February 1952, when a half-muffled quarter peal was rung at St Alphege.

While the council may have banned television aerials from its rented houses, it wasted no time in installing TV sets in schools so pupils could watch the coronation of Queen Elizabeth II.

The issuing of a coronation mug to every child was also approved, as was a special train to take schoolchildren to London to see the street decorations. Owing to the limited capacity of the Assembly Hall, the Coronation Ball was instead held at Lyndon School. Every baby born of the big day was given a Coronation crown (five shillings).

Bragg Brothers builders erected a triumphal arch in Park Road, while public buildings everywhere were emblazoned with bunting made by working parties in schools, youth clubs and Women's Institutes.

However, the biggest celebrations of the decade by far came when Solihull welcomed its first-ever royal visitor – the Queen's sister, on 11 March 1954 – Charter Day.

After years of deliberation, Solihull Council had in February 1951 agreed to petition the King for a charter of incorporation to acquire the coveted borough status, the population having by then risen to nearly 70,000. Princess Margaret was chosen to bestow the honour in person.

Around 100,000 people thronged the streets along which the princess was to ride in her limousine from Solihull railway station, with dome gathering at 6.30am.

"Even the sun came out to welcome Princess Margaret," headlined the Solihull News.

At a glittering reception inside Shirley Odeon, the princess presented council chairman Coun R Douglas Cooper with a jewel for Solihull's own crown – the coveted Charter of Incorporation.

She said: *"In the last 21 years this urban district has come of age and during that time it has been your constant care to preserve as far as possible the character of the countryside in which Solihull lies.*

With the enormous increase in your population, seeking new homes in peaceful surroundings, that has been no easy task".

In June that year, Solihull's first postwar carnival was held at part of the Charter Celebrations, bringing a staggering 40,000 visitors into the town and raising £1,000 for charity. One of the floats featured another royal visitor – Queen Elizabeth I in a sedan chair – aka Miss Mary Gertner.

Coun Wright donated the imposing ornamental gates at the New Road entrance to Malvern Park to commemorate the charter celebrations.

But just as with the granting of UDC status in the thirties, within a handful of years, even the new-found status was becoming outgrown, and councillors were moving towards the next rung on the local government ladder – becoming a county borough.

No politics in our town!

Solihull Residents Association has accused Labour members of Solihull Council of introducing politics into council work...

"We are so strongly opposed to the introduction of politics into local affairs that we must express disapproval of the Labour members as seen from both floor and gallery of the Council Chamber," the Association said.

Still, there was no stemming the tide, as the principles national government spread downwards into the lower rungs of local government.

In May 1953, Solihull Conservative and Unionist Association adopted a candidate for the first time rather than carrying on the practice of supporting independent candidates being opposed by socialist nominees. He was Coun Wynne Thomas, who successfully defended the Olton north seat he had held since 1947.

Biological warfare

Shooting apparently was no longer considered the best way of exterminating agricultural pests like wood pigeons. Biological warfare was the boffins' answer, and in Solihull it reared its ugly head in 1955 in the form of myxomatosis.

Several local farmers have ... discovered diseased and dying animals on their land and farm workers have interrupted their work to put the rabbits out of their misery. Within a mile of Solihull High Street, infected rabbits can be seen pawing the air and their eyes in an effort to breathe and to see.

Down Hampton Lane, many have been run over by motor cars ...

Solihull's most dangerous road

Since the dawn of the motor car, Stratford Road through Shirley had been notorious as an accident black spot.

In the mid fifties, a long-overdue decision was taken by Warwickshire County Council to widen it through the heart of Shirley where it had become dubbed the "Mile of Death".

The scheme cost £150,000, but in 1959, MP Martin Lindsay was handed a 6,000-name petition calling for yet more safety measures, this time at Monkspath.

Plans for a Solihull bypass to alleviate traffic congestion made the national press in 1957.

A centuries-old Spanish chestnut tree standing at the junction of Lode Lane and Manor Road was in the way of the proposed route – but it could not be chopped down as a preservation order had been slapped on it. It would cost £8,000 – a small fortune in those days – to take the road round it . . . if it was ever built.

Roll Over Bill Haley

The sensational film "Rock Around The Clock" which provoked near-riots among filmgoers at its showing up and down the country will not be shown next week at the Olton cinema as originally planned.

An official at the cinema said that the film had been withdrawn by a head office decision . . .

A cinema manager in the borough said . . . if there had not been such widespread comment on the disorderly behaviour of those who had watched "Rock Around the Clock" in other towns, it might have been possible to show it without trouble . . . but at this stage he felt it was best not to show the film at all . . .

(Solihull News, September 1956)

By November, however, the mood towards the film had changed. Fewer cinema seats were being ripped up by young fans and it was acquiring acceptability. Rock'n'Roll was here to stay; reported the News:

"Rock Around the Clock" is booked for a six-day showing at the 400-seater Olton cinema . . .

Mr G V Leedham, manager of the cinema, said . . . "In my opinion the fanatical reaction towards the film had died down."

And as a young man who prizes the reputation of his cinema, Mr Leedham is going to ensure that there is no trouble.

In their hour of need

If Solihull's wartime days of flying the red flag and friendship with the Soviet Union had not by 1956 long since faded into distant memory, the brutal quashing of the Hungarian uprising in that year effectively dispersed any illusions which might have remained.

Yet local people once again showed their true mettle in the face of oppression:

Solihull Council's decision to provide rent free a council house to a Hungarian refugee family has given the lead to local authorities throughout the country . . . the Council House telephone has been ringing almost continuously with offers of furniture for the Hungarian house and clothing for the family . . .

(Solihull News, November 1956)

The family, which had escaped across the Iron Curtain by walking ten miles through a forest patrolled by trigger-happy Russian guards, arrived a month later to a warm welcome at their new home in Broomfield Close – although they refused to show their faces to photographers and asked for their surnames not to be revealed for fear of reprisals against their families by the secret service.

Every schoolboy's dream shattered

All suburban trains serving Solihull and Shirley will be diesels after June 17. This is announced by British Railways as the first instalment in the Birmingham area of the policy of modernisation of the railways announced by the government more than a year ago.

(Solihull News, April 1957)

Modernisation on other areas would have been warmly welcomed by more than 40 occupants of railway cottages at Earlswood and Danzey Green stations – who had not been connected to a water mains and in 1958 still had their daily drinking water supplies, Sunday excepted, delivered in a five-gallon churn.

Solihull Council's Biggest Secret

Apart from providing a new civic centre, Solihull Council had secretly been plotting for two years to stage a major redevelopment of the town centre.

That fact emerged at an otherwise dull public inquiry into plans by solicitors Biddle, Dunn and Loan to continue using the former coach house and stales of a long-demolished Warwick Road property as a professional office.

Solihull Council objected – because, it emerged in September 1958, that it wanted the site for itself, as land to build 16 old persons' dwellings which would be needed for rehousing inhabitants of the town's central area . . . when 121 houses would be bulldozed.

Deputy borough surveyor Ron Richardson said that the town centre redevelopment plan had not been made public because "the considerable amount of administrative procedure" was not complete. For the appellants, Mr F Blennerhassett criticised the scheme as "a private secret of the council".

It was to radically transform the face of Solihull town centre as thoroughly as the new housing estates had ravaged the borough's countryside – and within two months, compulsory purchase orders were being discussed.

By autumn 1959, the road layout for the central area redevelopment was settled, and the council began negotiations with the Norwich Union Insurance Society, its partners in the radical scheme, who were responsible for similar developments in Croydon and Wilmslow.

The mind-blowing plan involved sweeping away all the old houses and shops in Mill Lane and Drury Lane, including Touchwood Hall, and providing new stores, with an ornamental traffic island in the middle.

A 500-space car park would be built between High Street and the site of the new Civic Hall in homer road.

Knowle was also to have a new central area, based around a "village green" in St

John's Close, with a library, car parks, district Post Office, a community centre and several council houses.

Empire building

Residents of Shirley and Solihull Lodge, many of who said that they moved there to escape city life, were therefore aghast when, in March 1959, Labour-controlled Birmingham announced plans to snatch a gigantic 624-acre wedge of countryside between Haslucks Green Road, Peterbrook Road, Trueman's Heath Road and Major's Green to facilitate slum clearances and rehousing programmes.

"The most efficient and practical method of developing such land is by its incorporation within the city", said the city's general purposes committee.

Solihull's mayor, Alderman Edgar Hiley, replied by condemning the bid as "completely destructive" which would result in a "sprawl" of the worst possible kind.

A total 4159 people signed a petition against the new-build scheme on their doorstep.

It was presented in June to Solihull Council by Richard Lewis, secretary of the newly-formed Shirley South Boundary Preservation Committee, and again to Martin Lindsay at the House of Commons the next day. The resistance proved temporarily successful . . . but Birmingham would soon be back.

As far as builders of the 1950s were concerned, they'd never had it so good.

A bird's eye view from St Alphege church tower shows Solihull town centre as it was before the wholesale redevelopment began.

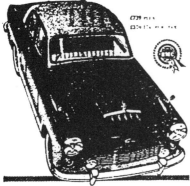

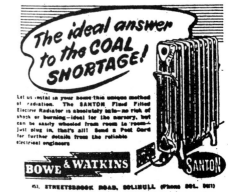

Chapter Seven

SOLIHULL'S SIXTIES REVOLUTION

1960–69

> So life was never better than
> In nineteen sixty three
> (Though just too late for me)
> Between the end of the *Chatterley* ban
> And the Beatles' first LP.
> *Philip Larkin*

After the avalanche of fifties development had surged through Solihull's rural tracts, fresh frontiers were to be assailed.

Then, it was bricks and mortar – now, it would be social attitudes rather than trees that came tumbling down, often by the week . . . and Solihull found itself somewhat more than a microcosm of the events that were reshaping British life and culture.

Mandy (Marilyn) Rice-Davies, who with her friend Christine Keeler was jointly responsible for the Profumo scandal that toppled the Macmillan government, came from Shirley: and a Solihull pop group reached the dizzy heights of the Beatles for a fleeting moment.

The passing of the old was reflected in architecture and the landscape: the multitude of time-honoured family businesses that we saw at the beginning of the century were swept away overnight and replaced by the brushed concrete, big stores and plate glass world of a brave new town centre:

> *Voices which last winter were raised in protest at the plans of the borough council to redevelop the centre of the town with new shops and officers were reduced almost to silence this week when a public inquiry into the scheme was held at the Council House.*
>
> *Originally there were 57 objectors. By the time the hearing was adjourned there were 13 – and three of those are likely to be withdrawn in the near future. Professor J S Allen, President of the Town Planning Institute, was told at Paddington station on Thursday morning that he need not attend the hearing to outline his criticisms of the scheme on behalf of objectors . . .*
>
> (News, October 1960)

Solihull's White House in Blossomfield Road and its fairytale gardens, once the home of Sir Robert and Lady Edith Bird. The house was sold in 1961 to Solihull Council to prevent it falling into "the hands of an undesirable type of speculator" and a three-day contents sale was attended by 1,000 people from all over the country.
It was demolished and the site developed into luxury houses and flats as White House Way.

Solihull's heart transplant

"The good old days" of Solihull town centre were condemned by mayor Coun Harold Shaw at the Civic Dinner in October 1963:

"Perhaps time has dimmed the memories of critics of the new Solihull and given beauty of their dreams

"With the demolition of the old Central Area one of the last eyesores of the borough will be removed. What other town of our size can claim to be free from slums."

For Coun Shaw, the reality of "old Solihull" had no modern schools, non-existent pavements, poor highways often flooded to a depth of several feet in heavy rainfall, streets sparsely lit by gas, water supplies from contaminated shallow wells – with fresh supplies from the council at a penny a bucket when they ran dry.

Many of the 200 residents of the timbered cottages in Mill Lane and Drury Lane agreed with him – and when they were rehoused on the council's new Bridge Estate in Lode Lane, they described their modern homes as "wonderful".

The first town centre building to be bulldozed was Georgian Touchwood Hall, which Solihull Society of Arts had tried unsuccessfully to preserve amidst calls for it to become a museum.

Also demolished was the Royal Oak Hotel where High Street met Drury Lane, and where "time" was last called on 26 January 1964.

Buildings, back gardens, mature trees – the lot were soon swept away, replaced by modern shop units with a central traffic "island" comprising ornamental fountains, and Beatties, a huge department store.

The old character had gone by the mid sixties, but Drury Lane unintentionally acquired a new one of its own, complete with micro-climate.

The passage beneath the new Beatties department store created a "wind tunnel" effect which would frustrate shoppers even on relatively calm days.

A new parish hall replacing the one in Mill Lane was named after local benefactor Capt Oliver Bird of Bentley Heath.

There are, however, those who still remember the "old Solihull" with affection and believe that tearing the heart out of a traditional town to this extent would not be allowed today.

Town clerk William Maurice Mell who took Solihull from its UDC days to county borough status and had been the prime mover in the town centre redevelopment died on 19 March 1965 at the age of 56, six months after his wife Dorothy.

The Mell Square shopping precinct which began life with a set of ornamental fountains as its centrepiece, was named after him.

Premium sites

By the sixties, development sites in Solihull were attracting top prices through the borough's assured popularity.

In 1960, land in Orchard Lane, Hockley Heath, land sold for a record £10,400 per acre, while a Bryant & Son showhome on a new Dorridge estate attracted 1,000 viewers in four months.

Radical plans to build a 10-storey block of flats in Copt Heath were turned down after a two-day public inquiry in 1963 and a scheme for a 23-story tower block next to

Old cottages in Mill Lane opposite the Rima Patisserie in a scene from Solihull's central area before everything was swept away during redevelopment in 1963.

Drury Lane looking towards Warwick Road in the good old days before the Beatties store would block the view forever.

Old Mill Lane looking towards High Street before it was all swept away in 1963.

A never-to-be repeated scene depicts the garden centre that once existed between Drury Lane and George Road.

Malvern Park in 1966 also came to nothing also after angering neighbours.

The new Central Electricity Generating Board headquarters in Haslucks Green Road, Shirley, withstood local opposition and was topped out at a ceremony in March 1966, when it became the tallest building in the borough.

But it was only in 1964 that the postwar prefabs – originally intended to last just 10 years – started coming down, those in Castle Lane being first to go.

Time for educational change

The new Solihull Technical College was described by an architect as "an insult to the town" in a pleasant parkland setting, violating local taste.

Yet it became so popular that when its doors opened for enrolment in September 1963, prospective students rushed for places "in such a way that it was more like January sales in a department store", said principal A J Parkinson.

Nearby, the £27,500 Tudor Grange youth headquarters and £10,500 running track was officially opened by education secretary Kenneth Thompson on 24th July 1961.

More residents again needed more schools. The Catholic Our Lady of the Wayside school was opened by Birmingham Archbishop Dr Francis Grimshaw in September 1961, with the adjacent modern church following some years later. St James Church of England school was finally replaced, having used the same building since 1830, and Woodlands infant school was built in 1967.

Plans for a potential change to comprehensive education, transforming 13 secondary schools into seven, were announced in 1966, amidst increasing calls for the scrapping of selection.

In October 1967 a teacher revealed that an unnamed Solihull child who failed the 11-plus examination was locked in a bedroom for three days and fed on bread and water as punishment.

Seven primary children also underwent psychiatric treatment for nervous troubles through 11-plus "cramming".

In January that year, 114 children at Hatchford Brook junior school had to resit the dreaded test – after pointing out they had seen the questions two weeks before in a mock test lifted from another local authority's exams.

Travelling in style

> Solihull station was graced by the arrival for the first time officially of a Pullman diesel express train, bright blue and gleaming outside, and inside astonishingly unlike anything we have seen on the railroad before.
>
> It will leave Solihull at 7.40am, arriving in London at 9.35, and will return at 4.50pm from Paddington, arriving at Solihull at 6.44.
>
> ... the mayor Coun Ted Lightfoot and town clerk Maurice Mell went on a special excursion to Princes Risborough and back. The train reached a calm 90pmh during the journey...
>
> The surcharges are enough to deter the joyride, but the people who have to go to London on business have now, at last, the means of doing so in superlative comfort...
>
> (News, September 1960)

The Blue Pullman, however, was not enough to save express services to the capital from Snow Hill via Solihull, as Dr Beeching's sweeping modernisation plan for the railways preferred the newly-electrified London Midland Region's New Street-Euston line via Hampton-in-Arden instead.

Dr Beeching had his infamous axe poised above the borough's western rail route, the North Warwickshire Line, which ran through Shirley.

However, a vociferous defence committee formed to keep it open and spearheaded by businessman Derek Mayman eventually proved successful after years of campaigning against all odds . . . despite a June 1968 demand by Knowle & Dorridge Young Conservatives for it to be completely closed.

Solihull's rail disaster

The twilight days of steam and the advent of diesels were a Mecca for the hordes of schoolboy enthusiasts who spent much of their summer holidays at local stations.

It was five young trainspotters and a porter at Knowle & Dorridge station who, on 15 August 1963, saw the impending danger when a nine-coach Pullman Express approached at 40mph – on the same line as a steam-hauled train pulling car transporters loaded with Land Rovers.

Nine-years-old Mark Ewell of Aspley Grove, Packwood, said: *"We all rushed towards the Pullman waving our arms and shouting to warn the driver of the danger.*

"One of the men was grappling with levers trying to stop the train. It slowed down a bit but then it crashed into the other train."

While the driver and fireman of the steam engine managed to jump clear, the Western class express diesel ploughed into the back of the car transporters, killing all three drivers on board.

At the subsequent Ministry of Transport inquiry, the diesel's brakes were described as "pretty poor".

An express goods train broke up at precisely the same spot two years later, losing 23 or its 60 wagons, striking the Grange Road bridge and showering the road below with rubble.

Modern miracles

Twelve days ago a Franciscan friar at Olton Friary died at Solihull Hospital. Today he is one of the fittest patients in Ward Seven.

Brother Bernard, a 39-year-old Scotsman and a gardener at the friary in St Bernard's Road . . . coronary thrombosis . . . collapsed an no pulse could be felt. £850 cardiorator just bought – defibrillator – enormous electric shock delivered to the heart – revived after heart stopped for seven minutes.

(News, February 1966)

The first "artificial kidney" machine of British design made for use in a private house was installed at the home of Mrs Carolyn Radnall, 26, in Prospect Lane – ending her twice-weekly overnight stays at the Queen Elizabeth Hospital.

(News, June 1966)

No place for women?

Old traditions die hard at the ancient village of Bickenhill, which is steeped in history.
    A tentative move by the vicar, the Rev Stanley Owen, to introduce "sideladies" to the 800-years-old church of St Peter found little favour at the annual parochial meeting . . .
    The move – an innovation successfully made in the sister parish of Elmdon – was rejected by parishioners after the vicar's initial suggestion was met with a stony silence. An all-male team of sidesmen was returned. (May 1962)

Meanwhile, Mrs Eveleen Middleton, of Stratford Road, became the first woman chairman of Shirley Chamber of Trade in 1962, taking over from Harry Sheasby.

An overdue visit

Solihull's royal patronage began when William the Conqueror gave the Saxon princess Cristina the manor of Ulverley in gratitude for her support.

However, Solihull waited seven centuries before it received its first formal visit from a reigning monarch.

The official opening of the new Civic Hall in Homer Road by Queen Elizabeth II on 25 May 1962 saw crowds pour into the town centre in the hope of catching a glimpse of Her Majesty.

It was exactly 10 o'clock that the Queen, who had awarded MP Martin Lindsay a baronetcy for political and public services in the New Year's Honours List, alighted from a train at Solihull station and stepped on to a red carpet.

She was whisked away by car to Homer Road, where she inspected a guard of honour formed by the Queen's Own Warwickshire and Worcestershire Yeomanry under the command of Major H B Haycock of Tilehouse Green Lane, Knowle, and three ferret scout cars, outside the hall.

Opening the door with a silver key, she was greeted by a fanfare from the trumpeters of the Junior Leaders Regiment of the Royal Artillery and officially welcomed by the mayor Coun J Leslie Shepherdson.

Her speech read: "*The history of Solihull is a story of steady progress from the earliest times, the pace of which has increased to a gallop in this century, until it is now in truth the 'town in the countryside' of its motto.*

"*But unlike the new town many of which I have seen and admired – your growth has been a spontaneous enlargement of the original village on the 'soily hill' where your magnificent church of St Alphege stands as a living witness of your long history, and is still the spiritual heart of your expanding township.*"

Speaking of Solihull School, the Queen said it was paradoxical that its greatest contribution to English letters might have been the governors' rejection of Dr Samuel Johnson's application for its headmastership.

The Civic Hall scheme dated back to 1924, when the UDC planned to build itself a "most ambitious" administrative centre, but were forced to scale it down in favour of a "pocket sized" Council House . . . which it soon outgrew.

A far bigger public assembly hall on a green field site was proposed three decades later, when councillors viewed Hammersmith Town Hall as a prototype, and invited tenders in 1958.

The Queen may have received a rapturous reception, but the canteen prices did not.

The aerial view from St Alphege church shows the central area after all buildings were demolished.

Solihull's first official visit by a reigning monarch . . . accompanied by the mayor, Coun J Leslie Shepherdson,
HM the Queen is shown a model of the new Council House after she opened it on 25 May 1962.

In June, visitors complained about paying 1s 2d for an ice cream and 10d for tea and biscuits.

It did not, however, need the aristocracy to officially open the largest single open-plan office in the West Midlands – the new West Midlands Gas Board headquarters by the town's gas works in Wharf Lane.

Completed in a year and three days from when the plans were first submitted, the £500,000 building was opened by gas board chairman's wife Mrs C Harold Leach.

The poverty line?

> *Solihull council house tenants who have good incomes, two cars and healthy bank balances were told bluntly this week: "Get out, and make room for people who need your homes".*
>
> *Several members of the borough council supported the view . . . that tenants in the £20–£30 income group should vacate their homes, to enable the council to house some of the younger less wealthy couples on its 1,500 waiting list."*

(News, June 1962)

Luxury council houses costing £7 a week for those in the £1,200-a-year income bracket in 1965 were completed in Foredrove Lane, Damsonwood, where a new-style estate mixing cheaper homes with the more expensive mushroomed by the end of the decade.

A rose by any other number

> *The total inadequacy of local house numbering came under rapid fire at this week's Solihull Borough Council meeting.*
>
> *One member at the debate condemned "pre war snobbery" which induced a householder "with any status at all having a nice name to his house".*

(News, October 1962)

A hostile takeover defeated

By 1961, Birmingham's bitterly-opposed expansion plans sought not only to build on virgin countryside next to Shirley but to absorb the whole of Solihull Lodge.

To much local display the Ministry of Housing and Local Government released land for 600 acres in Wythall and Solihull to relieve Birmingham overspill problems.

However, a major U-turn in March 1962 saw the Minister of Housing Dr Charles Hill reject the new-build plans on green belt grounds . . . leaving Birmingham to look to Druid's Heath.

And a "Victory!" telegram from Martin Lindsay in March 1963 lifted the gloom from thousands of Solihull Lodge residents who had been fighting Birmingham City Council's takeover plans for the past four years.

Protest leader Richard Lewis, by now a councillor, said: "It will I hope illustrate to those who doubted our chances of success that when public opinion is expressed, it can sway even the highest of decision."

Local residents did, however, lose one planning battle – a mass campaign against plans by Ansells brewery to build the Lodge pub in Yardley Wood Road.

A blonde bombshell beneath the Conservative government

International attention focused on a semi-detached house in Blenheim Road Shirley when an 18-year-old blonde model gave a press conference on 18 June 1963.

Former Miss Austin Mandy Rice-Davies spoke of her friendship with Soviet diplomat Captain Eugene Ivanov, who shared the affections of her friend Christine Keeler with War Minister John Profumo.

The previous day, Labour leader Harold Wilson had stunned the Commons with an attack on Prime Minister Harold Macmillan over the national security implications, while the decline in public standards was lamented throughout the land.

Miss Davies refused to be photographed until a pair of adhesive eyelashes had been fetched.

> *"Eugene and I were great friends", she said. I adored him. He tried to indoctrinate me as a communist, but I was never asked to get any secret information from anyone.*
>
> *"I suppose I met him about 50 times. Christine Keeler told me that she had been asked to get information from Mr Profumo."*
>
> (Birmingham Evening Mail)

The rest, including her testimony in the trial of Dr Stephen Ward who committed suicide after being found guilty of living on immoral earnings, is not only history. It made it.

Slimmed down Solihull

Solihull became a county borough on 1 April 1964, although the "upgrade" saw it trimmed down to size.

Boundary changes saw it lose Hockley Heath, Dickens Heath, Tidbury Green and the still-problematic Mount estate to Stratford-on-Avon RDC.

Messages of goodwill were traded with Luton, for the two councils became the first new county boroughs since Doncaster in 1926.

A service of rededication was held in St Alphege church with a civic procession through the town and official luncheon and ball in the Civic Hall.

The following day, mayor Alderman Harold Taylor laid the foundation stone for the new Tudor Grange swimming baths in Blossomfield Road. It opened on 19 June 1965, 1,800 patrons turning up on the first day.

Tell Me When

Liverpool was not going to have it all its own way in the pop charts as far as Solihull was concerned.

A skiffle band formed in 1961 by young members of the 1st Olton scout troop with assistant cub mistress Megan Davies evolved into six-piece outfit the Applejacks, who were given a Monday residency at the new Civic Hall.

Like Dreamers Do . . . Applejacks acoustic guitarist Megan, aged 20, and drummer Gerry Freeman, 21, leave St Alphege church on 19 September 1964 after their wedding, as police struggle to hold back 3,000 jostling fans behind barrier in Solihull's own version of Beatlemania.
The Beatles sent a good wishes telegram from America and local 'beat' groups the Phantoms and the Con-Chords formed an archway of guitars for the happy couple.

Issued on Valentine's Day in 1964 was their debut single, *Tell Me When*, which received its first airplay from DJ David Jacobs.

More than 4,000 copies were sold within hours and the disc rocketed to number seven and stayed in the Top 50 for 13 weeks, earning the band TV appearances on *Ready Steady Go!* and *Thank Your Lucky Stars*.

Overnight stardom produced Solihull's own brand of "Beatlemania" on 23 March:

Within 20 minutes of the opening of the Civic Hall doors . . . 1,000 Applejack fans were inside. Then the doors were closed, with 700 screaming teenagers on the wrong side!

But they were not to be beaten by mere "house full" signs.

They shinned up 40 foot drainpipes and scaled part of the roof . . . they tried to get in by the coffeebar windows, some were seen squeezing through open windows on the roof . . . after the Applejacks had finished their programme the teenagers were persistent in their demands for more and hall manager Leslie Holmes had to lock the group in a room for their own safety . . .

Problems arose because three members, Phil Cash, Don Gould and Martin Baggott, all 16, were still at Tudor Grange school. Headmaster Arthur Munday said they would have to choose between education or showbusiness.

The boys' parents spoke Mr Munday and then asked the group's manager Arthur Smith what would their prospects be if they became full-time entertainers.

The sky's the limit," replied Mr Smith.

That clinched it.

Two further chart hits, *Like Dreamers Do* and *Three Little Words*, followed *Tell Me When*, but then the group faded into obscurity, performing on ocean liners for some years. A CD collection of their recordings appeared on the Deram label in 1990.

Real cool

When Solihull' first ice rink was opened by mayor Alderman Taylor on 21 December 1964, it had the largest surface of any English rink outside London – more than 16,650 square feet.

The refrigeration scheme involves more than seven miles of under-ice steel piping, and there were 1,200 pairs of skates and boots for hire, with 1,000 seats for spectators, a restaurant and licensed club.

However, the Cresta Bingo club above the rink, opened in September 1966, lasted only four weeks before heavy taxes on gambling drove it out of business.

The Silhill Hall affair

Solihull Council refused to buy the 14th-century half-timbered landmark in Broad Oaks Road in January 1963 – but instead it was snapped up by 27-year-old high-flying Birmingham businessman Malcolm Ross in June 1965.

His restoration work, however, went way beyond the mark and the council ordered him to stop.

Passers-by on 27 March 1966 were left stunned when they glance over the hedge – and saw a pile of rubble where the hall had been:

Sunday morning churghgoers stopped their cars and gazed, almost disbelieveingly, at what the day before they had looked upon as town's oldest and probably most taken-for-granted building.

Ross claimed he had come home early, found the hall damaged by high winds and decided to demolish it.

"Fortunately I had a bulldozer on the site ready to some levelling work," he told reporters. The hall was shaking, and we got to work on the walls, to make it safe by pulling them down."

Ross was fined the maximum £100 by local magistrates after pleading guilty to damaging a listed building.

Chairman Mr Hamilton Twigg told him: "You have impoverished the local community and have deprived us of part of our heritage."

For English soccer's finest hour

With the approach of the World Cup games "World Cup Willie" will be making his appearance in badge form on blazers and tracksuits -and a Shirley firm will be responsible for putting him there.

> *"Willie" is just one of thousands of different badges turned out by the Shirley firm of Bryant and Tucker at Stratford Road . . . one of the biggest heraldic badge embroidery firms in the world . . . producing some 80,000 to 100,000 badges a week.*
>
> (News, July 1966)

In the mood

> *Paint that glows at you from the walls; lights that change colour at the bidding of the music, and a clientele dressed in white.*
>
> *These are the mood ingreients of a discotheque starting . . . at a Knowle public house.(The Wilson's Arms)*
>
> *A room to the rear of the building has been converted to create a nightclub atmopshpere, and named the 77 Disco.*
>
> *The discotheque – the word means "record technique" is open to anyone . . . dancing is to a juke box . . . the music will also have an effect on the lighting of the room, for two flasher panels, which change colour according to the pitch of the musical sounds, are included in the decorations . . .*
>
> (News, December 1966)

. . . and all at sea

> *A former car salesman in Solihull is now receiving more than 1,000 fan letters a week. So many, in fact, that he is unable to cope with them all, and has had to ask his mother to set up and run a fan club for him.*
>
> *He is 21-year-old Peter Dingley . . . working flat out as a disc jockey on Radio Caroline South, (a pirate radio ship).*
>
> (News, February 1967)

As Mayor, Mr Wynne Thomas starts the 15th annual road race organised by Solihull Cycling club in Poplar Road on 12 June 1966. He was the only Mayor of Solihull to serve without being a councillor, having lost his Lyndon seat after colleagues selected him for the position.

The saddest day in Solihull sporting history. Highgate United centre half Tony Allden (centre) accompanied by goalkeeper Tony Sawyer, (left) and defender Tony "Spud" Murphy run on to the Tythebarn Lane pitch for their FA Amateur Cup quarter-final tie against favourites Enfield in February 1967.
Half an hour later, and Allden was felled by a lightning bolt, smoke emanating from his crumpled body in full view of horrified spectators. (inset)
Highgate United went on to become the Midlands' top amateur team in the early 1970s, winning a host of trophies under Shirley plumber Nobby Clark with players like Bill Tetley, Barry Williams, Dave Cahill, Doug Pash, Martyn Williams, Bobby Hope and Roger Shaw.
But they never forgot Allden, naming their clubhouse after him. Also, the top teams in the Midland Combination compete for an annual cup in his memory.

His mother was Coun Mrs Mary Dingley, of Hampton-in-Arden, and in later years Peter, a former Solihull School pupil, became better known as Radio 1 DJ Johnny Walker.

A glory dream shattered

Little Highgate United FC, members of the Worcestershire Combination, found themselves just two steps from Wembley, when they reached the quarter final of the FA Amateur Cup.

They landed a dream tie at home to crack London side Enfield at their Tythebarn Lane, Shirley headquarters on 25 February, 1967.

Favourites Enfield went 1–0 up in front of 3,000 spectators – before disaster struck from the skies.

A bolt of lightning blasted a group of five players, leaving brothers Eric and Roy Taylor, Mick Keeley and Enfield's Ray Hill suffering from shock . . . and Highgate's 23-year-old centre half Tony Allden with fatal injuries.

He died in Solihull Hospital the following day.

The replay was staged at Villa Park, when stewards were stunned by the attendance of 31,632, the vast majority coming to pay their respects to a player that they had never seen.

Enfield won 6–0, and reserve centre half Maurice Donaghy who took Allden's place walked from the pitch in tears.

Both Villa and Highgate donated their share of the gate receipts to a fund set up for Allden's young widow Susan, and after a memorial game against an All Stars XI was staged a total of £6,052 was raised.

Enoch's new fans

Enoch Powell's explosive "rivers of blood" speech in which he predicted future conflict between white people and immigrants in Birmingham led to his sacking from the Tory shadow cabinet in April 1968 . . . and support from unlikely quarters.

Around 150 factory workers at Joseph Lucas in Marshall Lake Road, Shirley, who might normally have voted Labour, downed tools for an hour in support of him, while several counterparts at Wavis Engineering walked out after a vote had been taken on the factory floor.

Solihull MP Percy Grieve, who had replaced Sir Martin Lindsay in 1964, described the speech as "sound and true" . . . but not "judiciously expressed".

Beyond Flower Power?

> *A group of grammar school students will approach people in the streets of Solihull . . . handing them small cards bearing words like "dewdrop" and "silken" . . .*
>
> *Their aim: to help people discover beauty in their everyday surroundings.*
>
> *Their belief: that many Solihull people are uncreative and lacking in artistic imagination.*
>
> *Sixth-former Neil Megson, of Links Drive, Solihull, has formulated a campaign aimed to bring enlightenment to the town. He is being helped by Bas Hermon (17) of Stonor Park Road, and Paul Wolfson, (17), of Broad Oaks Road.*

> *They have formed a society to be called the Knights of the Pentecostal Flame . . .*
>
> (News, June 1968).

It's too swish!

> *The new council suite containing a debating chamber, committee rooms and the Mayor's Parlour is "too luxurious", a senior Solihull alderman said.*
>
> *Edgar Hiley writes . . . "When one recalls the row we kicked up about the alleged extravagance over the old council house . . . it is quite surprising that not a word has been said about the much more expensive premises we now occupy."*
>
> *All the same, he says, the premises are excellent, and once the air conditioning ceases to give us the risks of pneumonia, all should function well.*
>
> (News, June 1968)

The new suite was another piece in the town centre redevelopment jigsaw, replacing the old Council House in Poplar Road.

Ulster in our midst?

> *Roman Catholic parents of young people in Olton have told priests at Olton Friary that membership of the youth club there should be confined to Roman Catholics to avoid the possibility of mixed marriages.*
>
> *The parents' fears came to light when efforts were being made to increase the number of active youth members.*
>
> (Solihull News, January 1969)

Waste and want not?

> *A refuse collector claimed that the generosity of people in Solihull had enabled him almost to furnish his living room . . . he described the high-class rubbish thrown out . . .*
>
> *Another collector, working in the central area, said: "People tend to throw out things such as vases, dresses and suites. Sometimes in good shape.*
>
> *"Shortly after Christmas we came across children's toys which could still have been sold at a good price in the shops."*
>
> *Another ashman said: "We get transistor radios and record players as well" . . .*
>
> (News, March 1969)

Stopped at the last hurdle

Twenty sixth formers who turned up to take their last A-level examination at Harold Malley boys grammar school in June 1969 were in for a shock.

Headmaster Roland Collins ordered them to line up – and inspected their hairstyles.

Four were singled out, handed razors and soap, and told to shave off their sideboards or moustaches . . . or be refused admission to the exam.

Two complied, but Stephen Hill, of Wychnor Road, and David Livingston, also 18, of Faulkner Road, both refused. The case provoked a borough-wide controversy and also made national headlines.

Having run the school in Blossomfield Road since it opened in the early sixties, Mr Collins had been viewed by many as a progressive headmaster, telling grammar schools to scrap Latin in favour of technology, dispensing with "old fashioned" speech days and prizegivings, and pioneering modern mathematics.

Under his guidance the parent-teacher association had bought a disused school in the Cambrian mountains of mid-Wales for £300 and turned in into a field centre for pupils, another borough first.

Opinions were divided. Far from being sixties hippy types, many said the pair looked quite smart and presentable. Others praised Mr Collins' disciplinarian approach and said rules should be obeyed.

Banners outside the old Sydenhams Garden centre in Stratford Road, Monkspath, on a snowy day in 1964 invites customers to think of summer blooms and order shrubs and roses. Sydenhams was eventually taken over by the Notcutts chain and the site was completely redeveloped in the 1980s, with the garden centre being moved sideways to allow a giant Tesco hypermarket to be built on the site.
The development did, however, allow for the retention of an adjoining hay meadow, ecologically important because it had not been ploughed for centuries and contained many rare old plants and flowers. The meadow is open to the public once a year but a scheme by the Warwickshire Nature Conservation Trust to move the part of it which was taken for the new development to a new and secret site near Knowle proved a failure when the plants refused to 'take' – a fact which underlines the vulnerability of such habitats. Ancient Shelley Lane – once the Kings Highway between medieval Solihull and Stratford-upon-Avon – still runs behind the Tesco filling station.

The row ended when school governors issued a statement saying that his action "might not have been the most appropriate" – and the boys sat their exams elsewhere.

Greater Birmingham beckons

The fifties ended with a takeover bid by Birmingham for a small part of Solihull . . . and the subsequent decade concluded with plans by the city to swallow it all.

Lord Redcliffe-Maud's Royal Commission of Local Government report of 1969 planned to sweep away the borough's identity _ and make it part of a Birmingham "metropolitan district" along with Sutton Coldfield.

A cut-out voting slip on page one of the Solihull News summed up Silhillians' enthusiasm for the scheme. For: 10. Against: 1,200.

Meanwhile, city leader Alderman Frank Griffin spoke of using land "from beyond Elmdon round to Tanworth-in-Arden" for housing Birmingham people. Meanwhile, the Board of Trade announced proposals for a National Exhibition Centre near Elmdon which would be larger than London's Olympia or Earl's Court . . .

The battle lines were drawn.

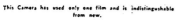

Chapter Eight

METROPOLITAN MEN

1970–79

Alderman Edgar Hiley retired in a storm of protest over the Maud Report as Solihull made it perfectly clear that it wanted nothing, repeat nothing, to do with being part of Birmingham.

Instead, the desperate borough council suggested merging with Sutton Coldfield and parts of Meriden, Stratford and even Atherstone and Lichfield if it could not keep its own identity under the sweeping local government reorganisation that was to follow.

The Tory government that replaced the Harold Wilson administration heard listened, and Environment Secretary Peter Walker said that not only could Solihull be saved – but it could take a chunk of Birmingham as well.

However, it was now the turn of the residents of Hall Green, Billesley, Fox Hollies and Acocks Green to express their animosity to absorption.

Their argument was also heard, and in October 1971 it was announced that Solihull would not have Hall Green . . . but Chelmsley Wood, the vast Birmingham council overspill estate built in the sixties on the site of a Warwickshire bluebell woodland, along with Marston Green, Kingshurst and Castle Bromwich – areas which had never belonged to the town.

Meriden was to be included, with the other former Solihull RDC areas of Balsall Common, Barston, Berkswell – and Hockley Heath would come back after a ten-year absence.

Coun Mrs Audrey Godderidge became the first and last woman mayor of the county borough in May 1973.

On 1 April 1974, Solihull became a metropolitan borough council and, along with Birmingham, Sandwell, Coventry, Dudley, Walsall and Wolverhampton, one of the seven members of a new West Midlands county.

"The Village of the Seventies"

The problem of Solihull's "shanty town" – the Mount – was resolved after half a century when around 100 residents sold out to housebuilders the Greaves Organisation which bought the 67-acre site for nearly £1 million in 1968.

It planned to develop it as a modern "village" community called Cheswick Green with up to 800 houses and its own village green, shops, pub and open spaces.

Prices ranged from £4,395 for a terraced house to more than £8,500 for a four-bedroom detached, with the whole of the first phase sold out in two days in 1969.

Quinton-born Alison Watson, 24, and husband John were among the first householders when they moved in from Bournemouth.

The new residents were outraged when in 1973, Greaves planned to bulldoze the 13th-century Mount to make way for yet more homes.

A furious Jeff Perry, secretary of Solihull Archaeological Group, attacked the Department of the Environment for allowing building on the site.

The builders agreed to a fresh archaeological dig, which revealed the foundations of a building and items of pottery, and part of the earthwork was eventually preserved as open space.

However, the beautiful six-feet-deep tree-lined moat was infilled, reportedly with asbestos, as the developers said that it was unsafe for children . . .

A showcase for the whole nation

The sleepy village of Bickenhill, where horses outnumbered the human population, became overshadowed by plans to build the National Exhibition Centre, a major "first" not only for Britain but for the provinces too.

Locals did not share the government's enthusiasm:

> *Gloria Greenbelt, vivacious blonde of the "Hands off the Meriden greenbelt" posters, will come to life on Monday wearing her karate suit.*
>
> *Gloria will lead a procession of cars, tractors, diggers and lorries in a rally, planned to protest against the erosion of the greenbelt and the proposed National Exhibition Centre at Bickenhill.*

(News, May 1971)

A public inquiry at Coleshill heard that the 310-acre site at Warren Farm had excellent transport communications being near Birmingham airport and the main railway line to London Euston.

The scheme involving seven covered exhibition halls with a show area of a million square feet was given the go-ahead by Peter Walker n November 1971.

Work began in February 1973 at a ceremony attended by Edward Heath. The complex was officially opened by the Queen and Prince Philip on 2 February 1976, when the first event, the International Spring Fair, got underway.

A marvellous start brought orders worth £650million, with Exquisite Jewellery of Lode Lane receiving a Canadian order for silver spoons worth up to £50,000.

The Queen also paid an official visit to Solihull in July 1977, when 50,000 people packed Mell Square to catch a glimpse of her, just a few weeks after celebrating her Silver Jubilee with street parties across the borough.

Meriden residents showed no nostalgia for the passing of the old Triumph factory on their doorsteps when they succeeded in blocking plans to build another major venue, the National Motorcycle Museum.

However, it was developed at another site two miles to the east along the A45 at Bickenhill and opened in 1986 at a cost of £1.75 million.

Mell Square in 1970. The centrepiece fountains had become an eyesore by the time that were replaced in the late 1980s by a futuristic-looking cafe when the borough council pedestrianised the precinct after giving it a "Victorian style" facelift with block paving and ornamental ironwork.

A typical potholed and unmetalled road in the Mount estate, where houses sprang up without planning consent and periodically caused major concerns about health. The estate was bulldozed to make way for Cheswick Green, the "village of the seventies".

All in one

The borough council was told in March 1970 to name the day for changing to comprehensive education and abolishing its state grammar schools.

The plans had been drawn up four years earlier and the changeover went ahead in 1973, despite the demise of the Labour government.

Single sex schools merged to become mixed, like Harold Malley and Harold Cartwright which became Alderbrook, and a new school for 11–16 year-olds, Langley, opened in Olton.

Olton Convent school merged with Bishop Glancey RC secondary in Whitefields Road to become St Peters.

Post-16 A-level studies were switched to a new showpiece Sixth Form College designed as a "mini university" with Hampshire headmaster Arthur Frankland its first principal.

Its opening in 1974 led to students at Solihull Technical College claiming their establishment had become a "poor relation" lacking refinements like chandeliers, tinted glass and a "purposeless" roundabout in the driveway.

A bid to merge the pair in 1993 was defeated.

Solihull's next charts sensation?

> *Olton pop group Hot Blood split up after having £500 worth of equipment stolen from their van . . . they have no money to buy new instruments . . . the group's agent, Miss Paula Bailey, described Hot Blood as "one of the best groups in the Midlands" . . . the Amalgamation from Hampton-in-Arden stepped in on Monday to fill the spot left vacant at La Dolce Vita . . .*

(News, March 1970)

Slightly less misfortune befell a band which regularly rehearsed at the Old Moselians rugby club in Lugtrout Lane, Catherine-de-Barnes.

Electric Light Orchestra fronted by Jeff Lynne stormed the charts with their single 10538 Overture in 1972 and went on to become one of the world's biggest-selling bands of the decade . . .

A cult surfaces

> *A 16-year-old Solihull schoolboy collapsed and was taken to hospital after being "kicked and punched 20 to 30 times" in the playground of Tudor Grange Grammar School for Boys . . . . . .*
>
> *The boy was said to have been attacked by a group of pupils at the school who call themselves "skinheads".*
>
> *The incident originated at a dance held at Solihull Youth Headquarters on Saturday night . . .*

(News, March 1970)

Dark days

One popular image of seventies Britain in the 1970s is of a country held to ransom by union bosses.

A power crisis in December 1970 caused by striking electricity workers blacked out one in four people in Britain and brought chaos to Solihull.

Local police were unable to make contact with beat officers and panda cars and donned fluorescent jackets to man failed traffic lights. Local dairy farmers' milking sessions were hit, stores ran out of candles, and the general manager of Beatties, where a mink stole "vanished" during one cut, personally helped 40 prams down the start. At Sunhaven Old Persons' home in Solihull Lodge residents were sent to bed early to keep warm. Even the Central Electricity Generating Board offices in Shirley used hurricane lamps.

A candlelit kitchen in a Mell Square flat was gutted by fire when it fell over. Solihull's newest primary school, Mill Lodge in Aqueduct Road, held its first-ever carol service by torchlight.

Pubs like Solihull Malt Shovel and Wayfarer in Hockley Heath used candles and paraffin lamps, serving bottled beers as pumps would not work. Blackout brought an early end to social functions like, in one case, a wrestling bout at the Civic Hall.

The marathon postal workers' strike of January 1971 in search of a 15 per cent increase brought a 100 per cent union walkout at post offices throughout the borough, while Tradescantia Trading Co of Drury Lane ran a private parcel delivery service at 1s 3d a mile.

Newly-married non-union member Rodney Scrivens, 20, of Hampton Road, Knowle, complained about running the gauntlet of pickets at Knowle sorting office and living on the breadline for a month, with threats of blacklegging and a "welcome committee" if he returned to work.

Teachers strikes were not infrequent, giving pupils at Sharmans Cross Boys and Lyndon schools a longer-than-expected Christmas holiday at the start of the decade.

And in March 1978, pupils at Tudor Grange who themselves walked out in protest at teachers' lunchtime sanctions and demonstrated outside the Council House were caned.

In 1978, 10-year-olds at Greswolde junior school were barred from their Christmas party because militant teachers refused to cover for a sick colleague.

Health workers dispute, car workers strikes, the army running antiquated green goddess fire engines in place of their civilian counterparts, not to mention rampaging inflation, all compounded to turn 1978–79, which saw the biggest cold snap since 1962–63, into the infamous Winter Of Discontent.

It was therefore somewhat surprising that Solihull MP Percy Grieve was actually "shocked" to see his 1974 majority over Labour doubled to 32,207 in 1979, when Iain Mills wrestled the sister Meriden constituency from John Tomlinson and Margaret Thatcher swept to power, voters by then having shivered for far too long.

Highway robbery

A fighting fund under the banner of the Tapster Valley Preservation Society was set up to oppose plans for the new Birmingham-Oxford-London motorway through Lapworth. And a mass exodus of Solihull luxury houseowners fleeing from the route of a motorway designed to take traffic around the south of the conurbation was predicted.

Nonetheless, the £16million Solihull section of the M42 was shown the green light in 1974 and the section from Monkspath to the M5 at Bromsgrove along with the M40 in August 1976, although the latter pair were not actually opened until the eighties.

Work on the long-mooted two-mile Solihull town centre relief road linking Warwick Road to the A41/M42 junction finally began in spring 1976 despite protests from Seven Star Road householders.

New wine in old bottles?

Changing tastes and styles again were reflected in licensed premises.

The Gardeners Arms in Solihull high Street was pulled down in 1971, leaving a half-timbered outline embedded in the adjoining building now inhabited by McDonalds It was replaced by an underground "dive bar" awkwardly named Captain Locker, after naval captain William Locker rather than an actual captain's locker, and now renamed Bar Nevada.

Meanwhile, an 18-year-old dispute between the council and brewers Mitchells & Butlers over plans to build a pub at the corner of Danford Lane and Sharmans Cross Road finally ended.

Permission was granted after a public inquiry despite objections from 1,300 residents and the pub, named the Sharmans Cross, opened in the mid seventies. Neighbours claimed that its modern design resembled Noah's Ark.

A class war brewed up at the Boat Inn in Catherine-de-Barnes, over a Davenports Brewery decision to banish darts and dominoes from its new-look lounge.

> *Angry regulars, led by 64-years-old Ted Mason . . . are outraged at this break in a tradition which has allowed pub games at the Boat for at least 50 years . . .*
>
> (News, August 1976)

Solihull town centre also saw its first wine bar open in 1976, Lord Byron's, named after the great Romantic poet who had local connections, and set up in the former premises of Solihull Seeds in High Street.

Another major alteration followed nearby:

> *Solihull High Street could soon became the "Mayfair of the Midlands" for overseas visitors to the National Exhibition Centre. West Midlands Taverns Ltd . . . is planning to spend £40,000 on converting the Malt Shovel public house into a "high-class entertainment centre" with a night club – to be known as the "Snooty Fox".*
>
> (News, April 1977)

The name may have had no historic link with Solihull, but in August 1978 voluntary pest control officer Charles Little of Highwood Avenue claimed his work was being hampered by Solihull housewives – who fed foxes on choice chicken and milk, encouraging them to have bigger litters.

More concrete jungles?

Fierce protest has greeted . . . proposals to convert . . . quiet country Earlswood into a "concrete jungle" housing 68,000 people by the year 2001.

Plans for the new town were outlined in a report published by the study group appointed by the West Midlands Planning Authorities conference.

The feeling among Earlswood villagers toward the proposals was one of unanimous opposition . . .

This particularly horrendous scheme outlined in 1972 came to nothing, unlike proposals outlined two years later to build thousands of homes on farmland around Widney Manor station, with a spine road connecting the A34 at Monkspath to the town centre and the 90-acre public waste tip infill site at Hay Lane becoming a recreation ground.

Fleeing Idi

The first party of nine Ugandan Asian refugees arrived at Solihull Council House . . .

They were greeted by officials of Solihull social services department and given cups of tea in the office of the director Mr Malcolm Wren – and also street plans to the borough . . . all the group had to leave Uganda without much money or many of their possessions.

(News, November 1972)

Mad dictator Idi Amin's loss, whose mass expulsion of Ugandan Asians was also Solihull's gain. Ugandan Asian Dr O da Cunha, medical officer of health for the town of Jinja, was given a new job on the staff of Solihull's public health department.

But actively praying for expulsion from Uganda in the mid seventies was author Denis Hills, whose book "The White Pumpkin" written in Dorridge described Amin as a "village tyrant" and earned him a long spell in prison.

There, he was threatened with execution . . . before international pressure finally earned him a reprieve and his passage home.

Terrorism's softest targets?

The IRA bombing of Aldershot barracks in August 1973 was followed 10 days later by two explosions in Solihull town centre.

The force of the blasts from two bombs weighing between four and five pounds each ripe out the front of the Bristol and West Building Society in Poplar Road and severely damaged the front of Lloyds Bank.

The bombs had been found by PC Terence Bailey of Hobs Moat, who cheated death by mere feet in the blasts at 10.35pm on August 29 and was treated for shock.

The News wrote: *So, this pleasant dormitory town of Solihull, where nothing ever happens, has been singled out by the fanatics for a blasting . . .*

The bombers obviously had a thing about the town, for they were back on 14 November 1974, striking the Solihull Conservative Association headquarters in Warwick

Road. Several party members had been meeting in the building less than an hour before it was rocked, again at 10.35pm.

Nobody was injured, although caretakers Fred and Doris Betteridge were treated for shock at Solihull Hospital.

West Midlands Assistant Chief Constable Maurice Beck attended the scene straight from a blast at Coventry's telephone exchange – leaving bomber James McDade dead.

Far, far worse was to follow.

A week later, 21 people were killed and more than 160 people injured, including Elizabeth Heaver and Diane Bird of Farmstead Road, Solihull, John Haskin of Wagon Lane and Alan Bennett, of Neville Road, Shirley, when blasts ripped through two pubs in Birmingham city centre, The Mulberry Bush and the Tavern In The Town, as McDade's body was being flown back to Ireland.

A warning telephone call was made to The Birmingham Post just two minutes before, giving customers no chance.

No longer satisfied with bubblegum cards

A Solihull woman spoke out about the wife swopping and sex games of the borough's "permissive professionals".

She claims her marriage (to a local company director) was wrecked after she refused to join a wife-swopping ring in a local charitable organisation.

The woman, who is in her fifties and has two children, lives in an exclusive Solihull road.

"There used to be a lot of kissing and cuddling and sex games . . . when it started I used to be so nauseated that I just walked out with my husband. But sometimes my husband used to go back, saying he had forgotten his lighter or something.

"What I didn't know was that he was joining in."

She estimated that about a third of the people in her particular branch had been actively involved . . .

(News, December 1974)

Invisible ink

A new method of crime detection which involves painting valuable goods with invisible "paint" is the brainchild of a Solihull man.

The "paint" which contains trace elements of certain metals can be detected by police, using a simple scientific device.

The scheme, which is being explained in the television programme "Tomorrow's World", could prove invaluable to the police in tracing stolen goods. The idea for the method came to Colin Bell of Yewhurst Road, Solihull, in 1968.

(News, January 1975)

All change at the register office

Two women, one of who has had two operations towards a sex change, got married at Solihull Register Office and rented a flat in Olton.

The bridegroom, Mr Ivor Watson, (25) said he wished that people would let them get on with their own lives. He and his wife Margaret (35) moved to Solihull from London when their secret was discovered by his employers.

Now, Ivor works at a factory labourer in Birmingham with other men who think he is a man.

Officials are now investigating the wedding because the registrar, Mr Spencer Towers, had not realised they were both women . . .

(News, February 1975)

Women in uniform

Having a "bobby on the beat" has taken on a new look at Shirley – with a policewoman as a permanent beat officer.

WPC Fred Walker, who has been with the force for about 13 years, is the first woman to be appointed to the job in Solihull.

But Mrs Walker is not the only policewoman to take on a man's work. In Solihull Police there is also a woman inspector, two women uniformed sergeants and a detective policewoman sergeant.

(News, February 1975)

Temporary policewomen had walked the Shirley beat during World War Two but this was for keeps.

Solihull's new £5million Homer Road police station replaced the old one in Poplar Road in 1970, when traffic wardens introduced were introduced in the town centre and Shirley for the first time.

Funky moped

Solihull's Boggery folk club, held first at a rugby club in 1969 and later at Knowle's Bank House, had acquired local legendary status by the time that its founder member and star act, a local singer-songwriter-comedian, had the Top Ten in September 1975.

The song *Funky Moped* satirised the popular two-wheel form of transport that droves of Solihull's middle-class teenagers used to get around town on a provisional driving licence.

The artist was Jasper Carrott – and it gave him the springboard to fame and fortune, topping the bill at the London Palladium the following January . . .

Please keep them on

Mrs Dorothy Wilkinson, wife of the Canon Raymond Wilkinson, rector of Solihull since 1970, was invited to join an ATV studio hen party . . . to watch a performance by two male strippers- along with clean-up campaigner Mary Whitehouse.

Asked for her opinion after the performance in September 1975, Mrs Wilkinson said she had been "amused but revolted" by what she saw.

"The men look so much nicer with their clothes on", she added.

Staying ahead of the Japs

Europe's most modern car plant, the £95,000 development at the rover plant in Lode Lane, opened . . . amid a blaze of publicity and mutual back slapping.

The plant, which will be used initially to produce the new Rover 3500 – code named SD1 – is the biggest single investment in the British motor industry since 1940. The new factory is large enough to hold all six halls of the National Exhibition Centre with space left over. . . a new £31million paintspraying factory thought to be the most advanced in Britain . . . can deal with 50 cars an hour . . .

(News, July 1976)

New books for old

From the cramped to the comfortable – that's the change Solihull's booklovers can look forward to when they visit the borough's new £2million library.

Choosing a book also meant overcoming a feeling of claustrophobia in the old library premises in Church Hill Road. The new building (in Homer Road) . . . is airy, spacious and light . . .

(News, October 1976)

Tickets please

Pay and Dismay came to Solihull motorists . . . with the introduction of town centre car parking charges. A glance at the surface car parks at the Civic Hall, in Link Road and George Road showed a distinct reduction in the number of cars.

Gone are the days of sitting in bumper-to-bumper queues playing hunt the space. Hunt the motorist is the game in fashion now.

(News, October 1976)

It doesn't always work

Bill Grundy's notorious Thames Television interview in 1976 during which members of the Sex Pistols used foul language was credited as the spark which ignited the punk rock craze, which reached its zenith in 1977.

However, no such meteoric rise to fame awaited folk band Blackthorn – who were banned from Solihull Civic Hall minutes before they were to appear in a charity concert in September that year.

Solihull's promotions officer Derek Johns said the Coleshill-based band were banned because of bad language from lead singer Nina Szitris when told of their opening rather than top spot billing.

Silhill Lake City

The Mormons are soon to move their headquarters into Arundel House in Warwick Road, Solihull, for which they have paid an estimated £1million. About 70 people will be employed at the Solihull headquarters . . .

Both the Mormons, properly known as the Church of Jesus Christ of Latter-Day Saints, and the Jehovah's Witnesses were condemned in September 1977 as "heretical" by Canon Wilkinson.

Yet the Mormons' national HQ has become a Mecca for people tracing family trees, as the keeping of genealogical records is linked to their faith.

Too young but in love?

Canon Wilkinson himself provoked a major controversy in December 1997 when he married 16-year-old Sally-Anne Williams of Campden Green, who eloped with her boyfriend Michael Slater, 20, an ice rink attendant, at St Alphege church.

Her father John said that he had never agreed to the wedding, believing that it could not go ahead as consent was parental required for children under 18.

Her mother Barbara said: *"I nearly collapsed when they told us.*

"When I heard a rumour that they might be married, I checked all the register offices in the area, but I never dreamed they would be allowed to marry in church."

But the rector stood firm.

"It is Canon law that if a child is 16 and the banns are called on three consecutive Sundays, the onus is on the parents to make any objection".

Meanwhile, Tanworth-in-Arden couple Timothy Roberts, a chartered accountant, and Christine Saych, became the first divorcees in the locality to have a church wedding when they married in the village on 1 April 1978.

New build and old

The desirability of Solihull as an corporate headquarters was by no means confined to the Mormons, even though many of the office blocks that mushroomed in the town centre provided difficult to let in many cases.

Solihull railway station's former goods yards became home to Broad Oaks House, a plush office suite which became a landmark by virtue of its garish tinted windows. It was let to Leyland Cars in 1977.

The council bought 14th-century Chester House in High Street, Knowle, owned by the late antique dealer Peter Pickering, to restore it and turn it into a public library.

However, this consideration for historic buildings was not shared by all.

Shirley's Brick Hill Farm may not have been Silhill Hall or the Manor House and lying next to Cranmore industrial estate was certainly no tourist attraction, yet it was 200 years old and a listed building.

There was outrage when Bryant Samuel Investments Ltd. bulldozed it in late summer 1978 to make way for warehousing, ignominiously tipping the rubble into the old clay pit at the rear.

A new battle for conservationists loomed as £30million development plans for the airport at Elmdon were announced.

In 1977 yet another public appeal was launched to save Solihull's Manor House, this time for £22,000 to save the face of the building affectionately known as the "old lady in the High Street". Mishap fell, apparently, when the wind caught scaffolding shielding the works.

The hot dry summer of 1975 was followed by the heatwave of 1976, as evident when Olton Mere took on a seaside appearance complete with beach as its water levels evaporated, delighting local eight-year-old Mark Shepherd. As July temperatures reached the 90s making Solihull hotter than Hawaii, Severn Trent banned the use of hosepipes and garden sprinklers. Trees and shrubs at Notcutts Garden centre in Monkspath perished as garden furniture sales rocketed . . .

The massive scheme involving a 270-acre expansion of the airport with a completely new terminal to replace the by-then inadequate prewar facilities was announced in 1979.

It would also involve the loss of Marston Green golf course, Chapel House Farm, and Marston Hall, an Elizabethan manor house described as an "architectural gem".

Chapter Nine

BOOM AND BUST
1980–89

The erosion of a little piece old Solihull made world news at the start of the new decade, although not in the way that anyone intended.

Work on building the Cranmore-Widney mini-town was well under way as green fields succumbed once more to bricks and mortar, but it still raised a few eyebrows when a demolition contractor arrived at 200-year-old Monkspath Hall in Stratford Road, Monkspath, on Sunday, 30 November, 1980. reducing it to rubble inside 20 minutes.

But in this instance, the owner, Solihull Council, was not to blame.

Demolition contractor D Doyle (Birmingham) Ltd had been hired to flatten a series of cowsheds at the back.

Instead, director Patrick Keenan, of Perry Barr began work a day early, misread his instructions . . . and instead knocked the hall itself down, despite protests from onlookers.

His error made news copy around the globe, with at least one newspaper in the United States describing the former farmhouse as a palatial mansion.

Keenan's actions were described as "stupidity and carelessness" when he appeared before Warwick Crown Court the following May, being fined £1,500 after pleading guilty to executing unauthorised works for the demolition of an existing building.

Judge Michael Harrison Hall told him: "You get on a site, let yourself loose with a bulldozer without having looked at the plans, without having read any instructions and you start to pull down the wrong building.

"Somebody suggests it is the wrong building and you do not look at your plans, you just carry on".

The company was also fined £2,000 plus costs.

There followed a seven-year legal battle which ended when the High Court ordered the firm's insurance company to pay the full costs of rebuilding the hall to its original specifications. It was then resold as a private house.

The cowsheds, incidentally, are still there.

The wrong way to make a fast buck

Horrific scenes greeted RSPCA inspectors when they visited Elvers Green Farm in Knowle and found 5,000 Greek tortoises crammed into nine wooden trailers.

Many of the tortoises were dead and their bodies left in a sickening state.

The discovery led to Tyseley pet shop owner Brian Williams, 48, and his son Paul, both from Balsall Common, each fined £350 by Solihull magistrates in March 1980.

The great survivor. Monkspath Hall farmhouse lies in ruins after a demolition contractor sent to knock down dilapidated outbuildings in 1980 chose the house instead. After a lengthy battle to win compensation, Solihull Council had it rebuild as near as possible to the original design.

For the defence, vet John Leach said that only one per cent of tortoises brought to Britain survived and that despite their suffering, those in the trailer had adequate food and water.

The pair, who had once exported deer for the Queen, did not have their pet shop licence revoked.

However, the case caused widespread anger and led to a Government ban on the importation of tortoises from the Mediterranean countries, thereby making this once-common garden pet a real enthusiast's item with specimens fetching hundreds of pounds.

Dancing in the street

> *Jubilant residents of Colebrook Croft in Shirley have won their battle to celebrate the Queen Mother's birthday with a street party.*
>
> *And appropriately the delighted residents received the news on the Queen Mother's official (80th) birthday on Tuesday – from Euro MP John Taylor who had taken up their cause.*
>
> *Three months ago West Midlands County Council refused permission for the street party, saying the cul-de-sac could not be closed for the afternoon as it would inconvenience some residents and need police supervision.*
>
> *But . . . the residents application was reconsidered after a special plea by*

Mr Taylor, who is also county councillor for Shirley, and it was decided that
the event was "a good community activity".

(News, July 1980)

When Prince Charles opened Solihull's new £1.3million magistrates court in June 1981,
a month before the whole borough went wild with street parties in celebration of his
marriage to Lady Diana Spencer, crowds of flagwaving well wishers turned out to cheer
him.

Among them was seven-years-old Samantha Kemp of Stratford Road, Shirley, who
presented him with a hand-painted plate as a wedding gift.

Asked why his bride-to-be was not with him, Charles replied: "I try to explain to
people that it is not altogether easy for her to do everything that I do just at this particular
point in time." Never was a truer word spoken?

The real emergency?

Solihull's hard-pressed ambulance service is having to cope with
"unreasonable" demands from the public, community health council
members were told . . .

Colin Jackson, area administrator of Solihull Area Health Authority,
condemned patients who demand ambulances when they do not need them.

"One patient asked to be dropped off outside Woolworth's so she could do
her shopping and another patient actually paid a visit to the ambulance base
to complain that she hadn't been picked up".

(News, May 1980)

Star quality

Hollywood film stars may soon be moving into Solihull.

For the borough's fame as a choice residential area for the well-to-do has
spread as far as San Diego, USA.

In a real estate article about housing trends in Britain, the San Diego
Daily Transcript informs its readers:

"At Solihull, the prestige area of Birmingham, where homes are less than
20 years old, you could close your eyes and believe you were in Bloomfield
Hills or Beverly Hills."

(News, July 1980)

Schools under siege

The sixties baby boom was long over. That was apparent by the large number of
unused places in Solihull schools.

Whitehall told the borough council to cut them – and several schools were earmarked
for closure as a result, including Sharmans Cross and Malvern Hall, which was sold to
St Martin's independent school in a land-swop deal including the adjacent Solihull Lido
open-air swimming pool.

A massive parent power protest in 1988 led to a 500-strong march on the Council

House which finally scuppered plans by to turn Lode Heath into a Church of England secondary school, an idea mooted for several years with Alderbrook and the closed Sharmans Cross also considered.

Controversy erupted over a council decision to sell off school playing fields, including five acres at Lyndon, 4.5 at Langley and 1.4 at Light Hall, for development.

While some schools were being axed, others were bursting at the seams through their popularity:

> *Coveted places at Arden School, Knowle, are up for sale – prices start at £53,000 and with them come luxury four-bedroom detached homes on a new estate.*
>
> *A deposit of only £100 can secure a child's place . . . parents who bought their homes in Knowle village as long as 11 years ago are furious that any family moving into the new Bryants Tilehouse Grange estate can send their children straight to Arden.*
>
> *Since the catchment area for Arden changed five years ago, even children with brothers or sisters at Arden have found themselves without a guaranteed place at their nearest school . . . children educated until now outside the borough can be assured of a place at Arden when other parents reserve one of the new luxury homes at the Browns Lane development – most of which will not be built for several years.*

(News, July 1982)

Summertime 1980 and the living is easy for Mrs Lesley Alcock from Cheswick Green and her daughter Karen, aged two, at Malvern Park Lido. Solihull council closed the lossmaking prewar open-air swimming pool a few years later despite massive campaign by the future Coun Mrs Amanda Jenkinson to save it. Now derelict and in the possession of St Martin's school, it may be refurbished and reopened in the future.

But the biggest row by far came in late 1983 when education director Colin Humphrey produced a feasibility report on the reintroduction of grammar schools – an idea immediately slammed by headmasters, teachers and union representatives.

Many wondered if the Tory Government was behind the move, "testing the water" in true-blue Solihull at a time when the failings of across-the-board mixed ability systems unquestioningly lapped up by teachers a decade earlier had become blatantly apparent.

Tory leader Coun Bob Meacham said the plan was part of a massive shake-up aimed at tightening discipline in "sloppy" schools.

Yet parents everywhere gave it a big thumbs down, forcing the council to make a U-turn within months.

One idea in the report that survived was the placing of headmasters on short-term contracts – so that those not up to scratch could be removed at the end. The first to sign such a contract was Dorridge Junior School's Steve Taylor in 1989.

Another slice of Birmingham

Already having been given Chelmsley Wood and Kingshurst six years earlier, Solihull Council in 1980 agreed a deal for the takeover of 12,600 houses from Birmingham City Council, then also run by Conservatives.

Solihull took over the outstanding £51 million debt as part of the deal, designed to unify the north and south of the borough.

Solihull Council leader Coun Wynne Rees said: "It seems silly that people in Chelmsley Wood pay rents to Birmingham and all they get is repairs to houses while we are responsible for all the other services."

In previous decades, Birmingham had been accused of wanting to swallow up its smaller neighbours.

Yet Solihull became the hunter rather than the hunted when residents of Lapworth and Baddesley Clinton overwhelmingly voted against returning to Solihull in a Boundary Commission ballot in 1988.

Solihull International?

Many civic leaders expressed bitter disappointment with Whitehall's green light for the plans to expand Birmingham airport, which lay inside the borough boundaries, so that it could cope with three million passengers annually.

A world first included in the scheme was Maglev, described as "the train of the future", which relied on magnetic suspension to "float" 15 millimetres above the track. It carried 48 passengers between the airport terminal and Birmingham International railway station, but was constantly let down by power failures and was made redundant in the following decade.

The £62 million Birmingham International Airport was opened by the Queen on 30 May 1984.

She said that she had mixed feelings about airports because Windsor was so near Heathrow, but: "We regard them as necessary noises!".

An economic cycle turns full circle

Shock waves greeted the British Leyland announcement on 12 May, 1981 – that it was to close the Lode Lane Rover car plant sacking 2,100 workers and transferring production to Oxford. Land Rovers and Range Rovers would continue to be made there and a promised £200million investment would continue.

However, as the gloom of the early 1980s recession dispersed and the green shoots of the Thatcher boom years burst forth, the plant was reopened, employing an extra 8,000 workers – and making the Rover group ripe for privatisation.

Plans were also announced for Britain's first free port at the airport, where high-technology components could be flown in, assembled and re-exported without the requirement to pay duty. It proved a failure.

The property boom

It was little surprise that among the many new offices that appeared in Solihull town centre during the eighties was the new headquarters of mortgage company National Home Loans.

For while Britain was gripped by a housing boom, Solihull prices rocketed by an astounding 80 per cent during 1988, ahead of anywhere else, as the M40 link to London neared completion.

Cranmore-Widney, later named Monkspath and Hillfields, became first port of call

Libbards Farm in Solihull found itself surrounded by another bumper crop, this time luxury homes, when the Cranmore-Widney "mini town" was developed in the 1980s. The house was saved from dereliction after a campaign by Michael Dillion, Solihull representative of the Victorian Society, and converted into flats. The site of its predecessor, a medieval moated manor, is still intact in nearby Widney Lane.

for many new buyers, with its £2 million spine route appropriately named Monkspath Hall Road providing a swift link to the town centre and the nearest motorway junction.

The estates received two new pubs – the modern Chequers by the Widney Lane roundabout and the half-timbered Shelly Farm, with the conversion of a medieval farmhouse into Ansells brewery's latest flagship hostelry.

The bubble eventually burst, and Solihull's Citizens Advice Bureau reported marriage break-ups rising by 12 per cent as higher mortgage rates took their toll.

Other house owners were beset by negative equity as prices fell sharply, and many of the breathtaking gains made during the Thatcher boom years became a burden to many virtually overnight.

Yet more stores

The expansion of the 1960s town centre resumed when the council announced a £10million scheme to bulldoze 90 homes in George Road and New Road to build a 100,000 square foot store in the early eighties. The outraged 200 residents formed a protest group to fight it.

John Taylor, the future replacement for MP Percy Grieve, said: "There are people who still refer to Solihull as 'the village'. It certainly won't be a village if we keep developing like this".

George Road residents sounded victory celebrations with a street party when Environment Secretary Patrick Jenkin quashed the scheme in July 1984, while giving the go-ahead to plans for DIY centres on the site of Shirley's old BSA factory, and for Tesco Stores Ltd at Notcutts Garden centre in Monkspath. The out-of-town retail park had arrived

George Road won only a brief respite, as the council slowly bought up all the homes to ensure there was no opposition when they revised their plans. A giant Safeway store ended up on the site.

At one stage it was suggested that a better use for the Civic Hall – by 1982 was losing money as the Library Theatre took away bookings – would be as a supermarket, hotel or office block.

It was eventually privatised and became the Solihull Conference and Banqueting Centre with a £230,000 facelift.

Details of a multi-million-pound expansion on the main town centre car park between High Street and Homer Road were put announced by the council in April 1989.

The development, named Touchwood Court after the old hall in Drury Lane, involved a series of two-level shopping malls with both big and little stores, interlocking pathways and civic squares and even an orangery.

The scheme, however, was put on ice as the national economy suffered a downturn in the late eighties and the council's backers disappeared. It resurfaced at periodic intervals during the nineties to little avail.

In the drink

For years Shirley doctor Chris Stockdale was hardly out of the news, raising cash for charity with a series of marathon swims.

Swimming the English Channel first in 1977, four years later he beat his own record

Battle-hardened soldiers in the Falkland Islands were mystified by the parcels they received from "Shirley from Shirley" . . . and were reduced to tears when they heard that anonymous Solihull schoolgirls had given up their crisps and snacks to help fill them. The kind-hearted children were later unmasked as Susie Clear, nine, sister Nichola, 11, and Leanne Turgoose, nine, pupils of Shirley Heath School, and "Shirley" was Mrs Shirley Brown, who later founded the Green Belt Defenders pressure group (standing behind).

They all fall together...Grantley House, Pendrell House and Duntley House, three of the high-rise tower blocks built in Chelmsley Wood in the 1960s, were blown up with 250 kilos of explosive after being condemned as uneconomic to repair. Pub landlord Ken Nye won a mayor's charity draw for the right to push the button on 26 February 1989. Such flats were based on a prototype in the South of France but proved somewhat less popular in Britain.

Solihull Mayor Coun Richard Lewis was stunned when Labour's Coun Jim Ryan grabbed the borough mace and waved it during a debate at the full council meeting in January 1988 on the planned coal mine at Berkswell, an action portrayed by Evening Mail cartoonist Whittock.
Coun Ryan said it was wrong that the council should give £100,000 to defend areas represented by senior Tory councillors when nothing was being done to help Bickenhill parish council fight green belt development which residents opposed.
Coun Ryan was at one stage temporarily thrown out of the Labour group for his strong stand in favour of protecting the green belt against developments like the mine and a planned super stadium by the National Exhibition Centre as part of Birmingham's failed bid to host the 1992 Olympic Games.

One, twice, three times a lady – that's Mavis Lewis, whose husband Richard was Solihull's first citizen for a record three occasions – 1981–82, 1987–88 and again in 1982. Coun Lewis was elected in 1964 as an independent sponsored by Shirley Residents Association and served until 1976. He returned as a Conservative in 1978 and represented Shirley again until 1994.

when he completed the crossing in 15 hours 56 minutes.

Later feats including a cycle ride to Folkestone followed by a cross-Channel swim and a run back to Solihull!

Also, former Solihull School pupil Adrian Ellison, 25, from Hampton Road, Knowle, struck gold at the 1984 Olympics when he coxed the British rowing crew to victory on California's Lake Caritas.

And disabled yachtsman Mike Spring, aged 39, of Portway Close, Solihull, whose leg had been paralysed by a road accident, raised £40,000 for the Pain Relief Foundation by staging a 2,500-mile lone voyage to the Azores and back lasting three months in 1983.

Dubbed Captain Courageous, he married transatlantic sailor Susie Young from Tunbridge Wells who he met after starring on TV's "This Is Your Life".

The Falklands Factor

Solihull sailor Jon Courtney, 18, from Bramcote Drive, was given just five hours notice to pack and join the HMS Hermes, the flagship of the South Atlantic task force which set out to liberate the Falkland Islands after the Argentine invasion f April 1982.

Other local lads were soon in the thick of the action. Stuart Mounty, 19, a weapons engineer mechanic, from Daylesford Road, survived the bombing on HMS Glasgow while Andrew Guggeon escaped injury when HMS Sir Galahad was hit. Mark Bramwell, 19, of Willow Drive, Cheswick Green, cheated death when HMS Ardent was struck and 22 lives were lost.

Mark Richard, 20, of Castle Lane, Hobs Moat, who was checking equipment on Sir Galahad when it was bombed at Bluff Cove, turning him into a human fireball leaving 38 per cent burns, was left with a crippled right hand and numerous operations.

Back home, local folk showed their support where they could:

Argentinian honey has been withdrawn from the shelves of a Knowle health food shop in protest over the Falklands invasion. Patriotic shop owner Mrs Shirley Randle hopes to sting the Argentinian economy by refusing to sell the honey.

Argentina also pulled out of the cricket World Cup – cancelling their game against Fiji at Knowle & Dorridge's Station Road ground on 16 June.

Rebels with a cause

Council plans to close Richmond House children's home at Olton to save money, with youngsters being fostered out instead, met with unexpected opposition – from the youngsters themselves.

Backed by the National Association of Young People In Care, the 14 residents claimed that the policy committee was wrong to make the decision without consulting them.

Many were young offenders and said that the quality of care that they had received there had put them back on the straight and narrow.

They took the borough council to the High Court and won an injunction in September 1983 preventing the closure – but conceded defeat when a social services review showed them they would be better off elsewhere.

True bluechip Solihull

Widespread local opposition greeted plans for a California-style high technology industrial estate on farmland near the National Exhibition Centre announced in January 1983.

With Solihull's splendid road-rail-air connections making it an ideal choice for such speculative developments, the West Midlands County Council bought 92 acres of land at Birchcroft Farm in Blackfirs Lane, Marston Green for the purpose. But Solihull Council, which publicly pledged to defend the green belt to the last, was absolutely furious when the Government approved the first 148 acres in 1985.

The council fought the developers, Arlington Securities, at a lengthy and expensive public inquiry at the Council House.

Amidst claims that 8,000 jobs would be created, however, Environment Secretary Nicholas Ridley gave the go-ahead to the bitterly-opposed scheme.

That prompted valiant little Bickenhill parish council to "go it alone" and take the case for the protesters to the High Court as a last-ditch bid which also failed.

Parish chairman Coun Malcolm Sheasby later slated Solihull Council as being "two faced" for sending the mayor to open the first stage of the development in 1987. But much worse was to follow.

In January, 1988, the Birmingham Evening Mail obtained secret documents which showed that the borough council had agreed to spend £1million on buying Valentines and Sidenhales farms in Illshaw Heath for its very own "silicon valley" high-technology estate . . . despite the local authority's earlier opposition to the Bickenhill scheme.

Hypocrisy, shouted critics, but the council pressed ahead with the scheme, named the Blythe Valley Business Park, in conjunction with a private developer, later "watering down" the "high technology only" clause, although an actual start was not made until 1997.

Having a Whale of a time

While the council itself was now planning to build an industrial park on green fields, Solihull businessman Mike Fisher was collecting awards from the Royal Society for the Protection of Birds for his private wetland nature reserves a few miles further down the River Blythe at Ravenshaw.

The private reserves lay in the grounds of his Whale Tankers factory, the tastefully-adapted Cow Hayes farm which by then had become Europe's biggest producer of waste disposal vehicles.

It appeared that industry, not elected representatives, had now taken on the conservationists' mantle in a bizarre twist.

Yet Mr Fisher angrily claimed that the council, certain members of which made it clear that they did not want his "metal bashing" in the green belt, had cost him more than £1million in export orders by blocking plans for an enlarged car park before a Department of the Environment inspector ruled in his favour.

He later built his own "castle" . . . made from upturned tanker bodies erected on an island in the reserves' main lake.

Council planners again objected . . . but Mr Fisher pointed out that he did not need permission as it had no roof. He was right again.

Have a nice day enjoy your meal

Britain's first US-style drive-in takeaway opened in 1986 by Wimpy International alongside the £870,000 Shirley community centre which had been opened by Princess Anne the previous year.

This burger outlet later won a Solihull council food hygiene award for excellence.

A storm of protest greeted a government inspector's decision to approve plans for an amusement arcade in Station Road, Solihull, against the wishes of residents, police and the local council.

The George & Dragon pub in Stratford Road Shirley was bulldozed to make way for Calendars, a continental-style cafe restaurant and despite a campaign to save it by customers, the Crown at nearby Monkspath followed suit, replaced by a restaurant-bar complex called Jeffersons.

This particular stretch of Stratford Road was becoming known as the "Golden Mile" because of the rush for land by developers.

Solihull's soap dish

> Former Tudor Grange pupil Vikki Chambers is the shapely new interest in Coronation Street.
>
> The 23-year-old grammar school girl has landed a star role in TV's most popular soap opera.
>
> Vikki plays Sally Waterman, who runs the office of the Weatherfield Recorder, the local freesheet where former social worker Ken Barlow has been taken on as a journalist. Millions of viewers have watched as Vikki tries to keep her new unqualified editor on the straight and narrow.
>
> (News, November 1983)

Rich but lonely

Multi-millionaire Harry Ellard owned a Black Country engineering firm, a 100-roomed Warwickshire mansion Compton Verney and two farms in Oxfordshire.

Yet he chose to spend his latter years as a recluse living in a room at his rambling Solihull home, the Regency club in Stratford Road, Monkspath, which he had converted from a private house in the 1940s, and had added bits to it ever since without doing really much overall.

Details of his eccentric existence – in which he ignored his substantial collection of pre-war Lagonda cars, instead driving a battered old Austin 1300 – emerged when he died in Solihull Hospital at the age of 86.

The club, nicknamed Harry's Folly, was afterwards converted by Wolverhampton & Dudley Breweries into the Regency Hotel.

A showpiece multi-screen cinema later appeared on adjacent land – bringing movies back to Shirley following the earlier closure and replacement of the Odeon by a Safeway supermarket, and also the demise of Solihull town centre's picture house.

A bombshell for the refuse collectors

A major bomb alert was sparked off by two rubbish sacks left on the steps of Solihull Council house by an incensed resident, the town's magistrates heard.

David Merricks, (49), of Witley Avenue, Solihull, was so angry by an alleged failure of dustmen to collect his rubbish that he dumped two plastic sacks of refuse on the council's doorstep on Christmas Eve.

But when the sacks were finally noticed by police three days later, the town centre was put on full alert because of fears that the bags might contain a bomb.

Merricks, a steel spinner and father of two, pleaded guilty to depositing litter ands was given a conditional discharge for 12 months. Magistrates made no order for costs.

(News, March 1984)

Goodbye smallpox

Smallpox was set to be eradicated from the face of the globe in 1978 before a woman contracted the deadly disease through her work in Birmingham University's laboratories and died at the old isolation hospital in Catherine-de-Barnes.

The hospital was closed in 1985 and was scheduled to be bulldozed or even burned down to eliminate an lingering vestige of the virus.

However, the following year it was converted to luxury flats after being given a clean bill of health.

In the black

John D B Taylor became the borough's first black councillor when he was elected for the St Alphege ward in 1985 at the age of 33.

Barrister Coun Taylor, of Broad Oaks Road and a governor of Coppice Junior School, who played cricket for Warwickshire's second XI, replaced the late Coun Norman Green OBE, whose name was later honoured in the name of the Tudor Grange athletics centre for which he had long campaigned.

Coun Taylor later unsuccessfully contested Cheltenham for the Tory party at the 1992 General Election when racism reared its unacceptable head, but was later appointed to the House of Lords.

Not only was Coun Taylor often confused with John Taylor, Solihull's MP since 1983, (middle name Mark).

He also began receiving letters and telephone calls from girl fans of pop group Duran Duran star John Taylor.

A show ends in tragedy

Disaster struck at a Territorial Army display held during Camp Hill Rugby club fete in June 1986 at its ground in Haslucks Green Road, Shirley.

A smoke flare exploded killing 23-year-old Private Martin Weston from Marston

Green, at a moment when the sergeant and platoon commander were Saudi to be temporarily absent.

Private Mark Wilson, 21, from Lapworth, later appeared on a charge of unlawful killing before Coventry magistrates, but the case was dismissed.

His defence maintained that he had not been negligent in handling the flare.

Tin can alley

A "tin can" award is to be given to the Foster Brothers clothing chain for the design of its £17million distribution centre in Solihull.

The award, an old tin can painted bright pink and mounted on a plinth – is to be presented to the national menswear chain by Solihull Ratepayers Association which says that the 56-feet-tall steel building with 300,000 square feet of floorspace is the ugliest in the West Midlands.

Association vice chairman Coun Trevor Eames (a prominent green belt and environmental campaigner) said that the building on former farmland overshadows local homes and "disfigures" the approaches not only to the luxury Monkspath "mini town" but to Solihull itself.

(News, April 1989)

Not a paper tiger

Roaring lions at the bottom of their gardens kept children awake on a luxury estate at Solihull, it was claimed.

Residents of Lakeside Drive, Monkspath . . . have attacked the borough council for allowing Gandey's Circus to set up its big top on parkland near their homes without consulting them.

(News, July 1989)

Going underground?

Fears in 1979 that coal mining could take place around picturesque Meriden and Berkswell shocked residents.

The National Coal Board has been surveying land and drilling boreholes – in a search for new coal seams.

Nothing more was heard, and the residents eagerly believed that all had gone away . . . until 1985, when plans for a "super pit" to tap the rich but deep the South Warwickshire Prospect were unveiled.

Under the National Coal Board plans, 2,000 mineworkers and 700 builders would construct the £400 million pit at Hawkhurst Moor over 11 years.

At least 165 million tonnes of coal would be extracted before the middle of the 21st century, with half a million tonnes of slag each year. The pithead would cover a whopping 70 acres.

Solihull's planning chairman Coun Grahame Boakes summed up the mood of residents when he publicly said the council would do anything "legal or illegal" to stop the pit going ahead, and called for the NCB to be disbanded.

Coal board chief Ian MacGregor added fuel to the flames when he said locals should be proud of their new pit which would create 2,500 permanent jobs . . .

More than 10,000 residents fearing homes being blighted by subsidence signed a petition and by the time the unavoidable public inquiry began in 1989, major local vehicle builders Massey Ferguson and Austin Rover had joined them, claiming that subsidence could irreparably damage their Coventry factories.

It was even claimed that the mine would cause subsidence at Kenilworth Castle.

As the decade closed, objectors held their breath . . .

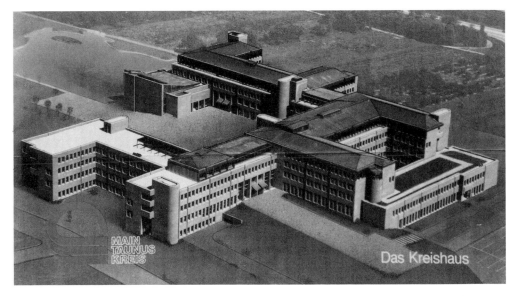

A new office block for Homer Road? An artist's impression of the new Solihull Hospital? Neither - this is Das Kreishaus, the council headquarters of Main Taunus Kreis, Solihull's "twin" district in Germany. Main Taunus Kreis has a population of 200,000 and its size is also roughly similar to the metropolitan borough of Solihull. Although Solihull Twinning Association was formed in 1978 with mayor Edward Barlow as a member, the Main Taunus Kreis link was not formally recognised by the council until 1990. Many exchange visits have taken place between the two.

Chapter Ten

SOMETHING BORROWED, SOMETHING
BLUE . . . BUT GETTING LESS SO
1990–

Solihull found itself thrust into the national limelight only a few days into the nineties, again for the wrong reason.

Senior borough council officers received a telephone call from the local office of the Birmingham Evening Mail shortly after 9am on 11 January, advising them of the page one splash that was to run that night.

Evidence had been uncovered of council employees running a pornographic film lending library from their place of work, possibly the most sensitive location of all as far as the local authority was concerned.

Stunned but intrigued, the officers were then horrified to be told the location of the illicit £1-a-day lending service . . . the chapel of rest at Robin Hood cemetery.

Two ushers, known only as Big John and Little John, were behind the racket, it was said.

As sub editors laid out the front page, the council officers made a series of hasty telephone calls . . . to the West Midlands Police vice squad.

Around noon, several strangers dressed in black mingled with mourners at a funeral service. At a timely moment, they pounced.

The vice squad seized a substantial number of video tapes, mainly pirate copies of legal films, and only a small proportion were found to be pornographic.

Little John, who had earlier apologised to an undercover reporter for the dialogue on one blue movie being in German, and Big John, who was subsequently fined by town magistrates, quickly parted company with the borough council . . .

A tax on all

"We can't pay, we won't pay, smash the Tory poll tax!" was the cry from rent-a-mob demonstrators outside Solihull magistrates court in the summer of 1990 as the tiny minority of borough residents who refused to pay strived to drag out proceedings against them.

The new community charge, payable by all adult residents and designed to replace the old rating system whereby property was taxed, seemed doomed from the start:

> *Worried poll tax payers are flooding into Solihull's Citizens Advice Bureau*
> *for help on how to cope . . .*
>   *Two weeks after Solihull Council set the borough's community charge at*
> *£389, more than £100 above Government estimates, anxious residents are*
> *looking for expert advice on paying their bills.*
>
>   (News, March 1990)

While Solihull residents chalked up a far better record of paying the poll tax than those in neighbouring Birmingham and indeed most other urban areas, massive public opposition led to the Government replacing it by a new Council Tax.

Carnage on the M42

The blackest day on Solihull roads came on 6 November 1990, when an articulated lorry carrying 20 tons of steel bars ploughed into the back of a line of stationary traffic at junction 6 on the M42 in Bickenhill at 65mph shortly before noon and burst into flames.

Six people died, including Sheldon clergyman Rev Tom Hodgson, and the lorry driver, Vincent Parsons from Newport, Gwent, was later jailed for three years after he was found guilty of causing death by reckless driving. Birmingham Crown Court heard that he may have fallen asleep at the wheel.

A new slip road was installed at the junction to prevent queuing.

Getting a buzz

> *A Solihull doctor claims he can prove that living near electric power lines is*
> *a health hazard.*
>   *Dr Mark Payne told a meeting of the Royal College of General*
> *Practitioners in Birmingham . . . that there was no sufficient evidence to*
> *advise patients not to live near power lines.*
>   *The Moseley GP who practises in Coppice Walk, Cheswick Green, said*
> *recently-published studies showed people living or working in a strong*
> *electric or magnetic field were at greater risk of depression, suicide,*
> *headaches, miscarriages, cancer and leukaemia.*
>
>   (News, November 1990)

The biggest battle won

"We are absolutely delighted by the decision".

Those were the words of Mrs Fay Cairns, secretary of the Berkswell Society, when she heard in February 1991 that Environment Secretary Michael Heseltine had thrown out British Coal's plans for the superpit at Hawkhurst Moor.

Mr Heseltine said that damage to the green belt outweighed the economic benefits. Local jubilation was indescribable.

After struggling with buildings adapted from an old workhouse for most of the century, Solihull finally gets its new hospital. The topping-out ceremony is attended by Mayor Coun Brian Chapple and other civic dignitaries. But no soon had the hospital opened in 1994 that problems began . . .

Sunshine brings the crowds out in High Street for Solihull Carnival in June 1992.

but another begins . . .

At the same time, Tory councillors slammed new proposals for an 80,000-capacity stadium on the opposite side of the M42 to the National Exhibition Centre.

Former mayor Peter Kellie said: "It will be eating up more green belt land, adding to the problems of an over-congested road system and attracting the undesirable element of football to the borough."

Nevertheless, Birmingham City Council and its deputy leader Coun Bryan Bird, backed by Aston Villa chairman Doug Ellis, pursued the scheme to build a £200million replacement for Wembley on the site, making an application to the Sports Council for National Lottery cash.

Solihull, the main opponent, was the subject of a bitter backlash from Birmingham when the bid failed in late 1995. But borough leader Coun Ken Meeson remained steadfast – accusing the city of arrogance in pursuing the project.

"Birmingham has fouled up," he said. "It assumed it could use its weight to rid over Solihull's wishes and was big enough to push the stadium through.

"It refused to listen to our advice. It had known about the problems with the site since 1990."

The city and Solihull, were, however, united in anger the following year when the Government rejected plans to hold the much-vaunted Millennium Festival at Greenwich rather than the NEC, accusing it of a clear bias towards London.

Offside!

Football was not wanted in Solihull. That was the impression left with fans non-league outfit Solihull Borough, who wanted to follow in the footsteps of prewar Shirley Town and provide local residents with a quality non-league semi-professional team of their own.

After winning a battle to sell its Widney Lane headquarters for housing for £4million, it became one of the richest clubs in soccer, but had nothing to spend it on.

For every time club directors found a site to develop as a ground, obstacles were placed in the way, and the first team was forced to groundshare with floodlit Moor Green in Hall Green to maintain its Beazer Homes League status.

A scheme to develop their second team pitch in Tanworth Lane was defeated after overwhelming opposition from residents, with 12-year-old Rebecca Botterille from Baxters Road even writing to the Queen and Prime Minister to protest.

The club even once considered buying Birmingham City FC and using St Andrews as their home!

After plans to move to the Bluebell recreation ground in Chelmsley Wood in 1995 were scuppered, club directors looked to Birmingham's Birchfield Stadium in Perry Barr as a possible permanent home, while supporters strove to persuade Solihull councillors to try once more . . .

The council reconsidered the club's plight yet again in the summer of 1997 and earmarked two further sites for possible development as a floodlit ground – Hillfield Park behind Blossomfield sports club, a stone's throw from their old headquarters, and the Norman Green Athletics Centre in Tudor Grange Park.

But it was the club's old local rivals Highgate United who pipped them at the post to having Solihull's first illuminated soccer ground, their floodlights being installed by September that year.

Bulldozed

> *A mad bull crashed through the home of a Cheswick Green family leaving a trail of destruction in its wake.*
>
> *The huge bullock smashed through the glass patio doors just seconds after mother-of-two Rosalie Kenyon drew back the curtains.*
>
> *It charged through the lounge destroying furniture and the television, ripping a radiator off the wall . . . then it lay down for half an hour to gather its strength before embarking on another rampage at the Saxonwood Road house . . .*

(News, February 1992)

Solihull's metal guru

> *An eminent Surrey historian made a special journey to Solihull to investigate what he believed to be the world's first aluminium workshop – but arrived to find the Victorian landmark bulldozed.*

A real-life Solihull century . . . Edith Arculus, 96, from Shirley, the oldest surviving pupil at St Patricks CE School in Salter Street, Earlswood, and four-year-old Hannah Collinson, the youngest there in March 1997, helped the Bishop of Birmingham the Rt Rev Mark Santer officially open the school's £190,000 extension . . . designed to match the original Victorian architecture. Edith's family, the Hortons, have lived in the area for more than 200 years.

> *Cyril McCombe was invited to the borough by local councillor Brenda*
> *Otton after it was discovered the building could have been the base for the*
> *19th-century inventor James Fern-Webster.*
> *But when the party of investigators arrived at the Solihull lodge site, the*
> *buildings had been reduced to a pile of rubble.*

(News, February 1993)

Top of the form

> *The first Solihull school to come under the scrutiny of a new national body*
> *for school inspections has won top marks.*
> *Inspectors from the Office for Standards in Education, (Ofsted) have*
> *labelled Monskpath School in Shirley, as top class in a complimentary report*
> *on staff and pupils.*

(News, April 1993)

Primary school performance league tables heavily criticised by teachers but welcomed by many parents were published in March 1997 in what was the biggest public information exercise since the distribution of ration books. Top in Solihull was St George & St Teresa followed by St Alphege CE (which had evolved from the elementary school) and Dorridge.

The top comprehensives were Arden and Tudor Grange, which, along with Alderbrook, began investigating the possibility of having their own sixth forms once more.

Meanwhile, rural Tidbury Green School in Dickens Heath Road, which had been threatened with closure due to falling rolls, was not only reprieved but given a long-awaited rebuilding, its old wooden classrooms finally being swept away.

A barn conversion too far

Tom Gallacher gained planning permission to convert a barn in Eastcote near Barston into two luxury homes, one for his family and one to sell.

The subsequent problem was, Solihull Council ruled, that he had pulled down too much of the original building – and therefore had contravened regulations.

So councillors ordered the Scottish builder to pull down the second conversion altogether – despite his repeated pleas that he had spent £300,000 on it and his family would be left penniless.

Mr Gallacher personally addressed a meeting of the full council in 1993 and even wrote to the Queen in a bid to save his development, but to no avail. The local authority hired local firm PBM Demolition to remove the illicit house.

The demolition crew arrived in convoy with a large police presence on 4 May, as waiting newsmen gathered outside.

Mr Gallacher then made a last-ditch plea to the contractor . . . and with seconds to spare at last struck a chord.

Brian McGarry, a director of the firm, turned around and told furious council officers that he would not do it because it would leave the Gallachers destitute.

His firm was sacked and blacklisted . . . but won more than a few admirers when the story hit the national press the next day.

Many locals felt that while the council's stand against any authorised building in the green belt was admirable, this particular case was perhaps the wrong one to have been made an example.

However, another firm was hired and carried out the job, leaving Mr Gallacher's wife Jackie to write a letter telling planning chairman Coun Geoffrey Gibbons that she hoped he rotted in hell.

The council later summonsed Mr Gallacher for the cost of the demolition.

Green Belt Defenders

A group of campaigners dedicated to protecting the green belt from "unwarranted" development are staging their inaugural meeting . . .

The newly-formed Green Belt Defenders is an alliance of parish councils, residents associations and community groups, all aiming to protect threatened countryside. Organisers said support is growing among MPs, councillors and individuals.

Group spokeswoman Mrs Shirley Brown said: "Gone of the days when small and inexperienced groups had to fight virtually alone the ambitions of those who wish to develop and thereby reduce the green belt."

(News, June 1993)

The group, whose members had already acquired no mean experience in spearheading a successful campaign against plans for another "silicon valley" high-technology business park, at Portway near Earlswood, featured prominently and effectively in several campaigns against major developments, including Government plans to turn the M42 into a 10-lane "super highway" and a scheme to build a service station at Wood End.

Renowned but effective battleaxe Mrs Brown became the Arden Area Planning Committee chairman on neighbouring Stratford-On-Avon District Council and was actively fighting environmental issues until a few days before her death at the age of 61 in December 1996 following a long illness. Her Earlswood ward seat was filled by her husband Peter at a subsequent by-election.

Never on a Sunday

The 1950 Shops Act, which restricted goods which could be sold by shops on Sunday in such a bizarre way that you could buy a pornographic book but not the Bible, was on the verge of reform in 1993.

Solihull Council, however, ruled that it would maintain its obligations under the law and prosecute offenders.

Safeway was ordered to pay Solihull magistrates £4,500 in fines and costs in August for selling a packet of tea on the Sabbath.

The Evening Mail then carried out its own survey . . . and bought packets of tea from 50 borough stores the next Sunday. Only two shops refused to sell tea, but one of them did sell the reporter a bottle of orange squash, also a banned item.

Council leader Coun Ken Meeson wrote: "As my postbag is now fairly balanced between those praising the council for upholding the law and those castigating us for

Following in the footsteps of the Applejacks: former Tudor Grange pupils Simon Fowler, (second left) and Damon Minchella (far right), plus ex-Lode Heath man Steve Craddock (left) and drummer Oscar Harrison stormed the pop charts in 1996 with their band, Ocean Colour Scene, with four Top Ten singles and a million-selling second album, Moseley Shoals.
Lead singer Simon Fowler from Olton, who also attended Solihull Sixth Form College, spent five years as a reporter with the Solihull News before becoming a professional musician in 1989. Their first album, Ocean Colour Scene, was released in 1992.

Nineties man . . . was this Steve Heaven's idea of heaven or just a little piece of it? The oil worker set up home with his girlfriend in a one-room 22ft by 15ft converted garage in Arnold Grove, Shirley, hoping to get planning permission for a bungalow later. But council planners told him that they were having none of it, and he lost a subsequent appeal to the Department of the Environment to keep it.
"There isn't enough room to swing a cat and there wasn't enough room for a housewarming party," he admitted.

One for the Millenium . . . Vicky Jones stands in front of empty Sidenhales Farm at Illshaw Heath in 1997,
awaiting redevelopment as part of the Blythe Valley Business Park after being bought by Solihull Council is
a series of secret land deals in the eighties.
The farm was owned by Henry de Sidenhale in the early 14th century and there are still traces of a moated
manor site hidden in undergrowth. Fiennes Fairfax Wykeham-Martin, the last of a line of local landowners,
lived here until his death in a motorbike accident in Hockley Heath in 1984. He left all the surrounding
farms to their tenants.
Nearby red-brick Valentine's Farm was demolished following an arson attack in Spring 1997.

Here we go again . . . pastureland in Dickens Heath earmarked for a new village in the late nineties
awaiting the earthmovers as Solihull's countryside recedes yet again to fulfil Government housing quotas.

obeying the law, it seems we are in the usual position of not being able to please all the people all of the time."

Mr Bountiful

Solihull millionaire Tim Watts was named as Britain's most generous man in 1994 when he decided to share £17million between 100 key managers at his Meriden-based firm, Pertemps Recruitment Partnership. The cash was to be allocated in 1999 as part of an incentive to boost the company's £60million turnover five-fold.

Locked out

The clock was turned back to the days before the motor car in 1994 when traffic was banned from Solihull High Street. A £950,000 refurbishment scheme saw block paving replace the tarmac and ornamental bollards seal off the roadway.

However, tragedy was averted by less than a whisker after ambulancemen turned up to treat a man who had received a high-voltage electric shock . . . and found their way barred by a padlock until firemen cut through it.

Electrician Robert Whitlock, 24, from Quinton, was working on a fuse box at the Mackays clothes shop in August 1995 when he touched a live wire . . . and the 400-volt charge which surged through his body. He stopped breathing and remained clinically dead for several minutes before paramedics brought him back to life.

Beatties extended their store in a £6.2million investment, swallowing up shops beneath it in Drury Lane and blocking off the wind tunnel effect, while British Home Stores opened a town centre branch.

A hospital of our own – or is it?

Numerous calls for adequate hospital facilities for the borough were made over the decades, with many promises and false starts being made.

Eventually, plans for a £20million district general hospital were given the green light by Social Services Secretary Norman Fowler in July 1986.

By the time it actually opened in July 1994, providing Solihull's first 24-hour accident and emergency department, an education centre and children's ward, the figure had risen to £34million. Yet borough residents were delighted.

That year, the old workhouse buildings were finally demolished after at last falling redundant.

Yet within weeks of the opening, the hospital was plunged into crisis.

It struggled to fill beds and made a £400,000 loss in the first half of the financial year . . . and a deficit of £7.8million was forecast for the next. And the West Midlands Regional Healthy Hospital stunned everyone by saying that if Solihull Hospital failed in its bid for independent NHS trust status, it would have to merge – with Heartlands Hospital in Bordesley Green.

Local people from all walks of life were absolutely livid. It appeared that key services would be moved into the city, where access was dogged by worsening congestion on the roads.

The announcement sparked off a Save Solihull Hospital Campaign which cut across party political lines, being spearheaded by Labour councillor Jim Ryan and later having the town's Tory MP as president in an unprecedented break with Government protocol.

And in February 1995, Coun Meeson became the first person to sign a Solihull News petition against the merger. His name would be followed by 80,000 more.

The first axe fell just two months later with 40 management and clerical jobs going. The regional health authority then set up a project team to explore the merger possibility, led by the chairman of the Heartland NHS Trust, Harold Musgrove.

Despite a series of protest meetings packed by more than 1,000 people and overnight candlelit vigils outside the hospital, Health Minister Gerald Malone approved the merger in March 1996 . . . promising that Solihull Hospital's future was secure.

It would get a renal dialysis unit and outpatients clinics, and he pledged to preserve the round-the-clock accident and emergency service, but the children's ward and emergency services facilities ended up being switched to Heartlands, causing yet more local fury.

Insufficient airspace

Increased commercial prosperity in the Midlands led to demands for the further expansion of Birmingham International Airport, which was running regular flights to the United States during the nineties.

A gargantuan scheme to extend the runway across the A45 into Bickenhill, by taking the trunk road through a tunnel, met with the anticipated blowback reaction from residents.

Hard bargaining by councillors under pressure to save the environment ended with a compromise deal in March 1996.

The extended runway plans were dropped, for an agreed 29 years, and night flights were limited to 4,200 a year.

In addition, the airport agreed to 106 separate conditions including the award of £100,000 for what was believed to be the world's first study into respiratory problems caused by fallout from kerosene fuel.

But the £60million Eurohub terminal, topped out by Transport Secretary Cecil Parkinson in 1990, would be doubled in size along with the main terminal, to cater for ten million passengers a year in the 21st century.

The deal enabled Irish operator Aer Rianta to buy a 40 per cent stake in the airport from the seven West Midlands authorities and put £256million towards the expansion costs.

And the next one . . .

With new estates at Cranmore-Widney aka Hillfields and Monkspath nearing completion, Solihull Council was forced to look for more land to fulfil government housing quotas.

In July 1989 the planning committee had voted in favour of a new settlement on green belt land at the hamlet of Dickens Heath, with Coun Eames attacking both the Tory and Labour groups for their willingness to accept the quotas without a serious fight . . .

The demand for sites continued, and in 1994 the borough was told to provide land for 9,000 more homes by 2011.

Solihull insisted that the best way forward was to build a new community in the countryside rather than expand the existing urban sprawl.

The final blueprint for Dickens Heath was unveiled by developers in March 1997, with 850 homes comprising a wide range of properties with a main village square, three other squares, a library and community hall, a wharf linked to the Stratford-upon-Avon Canal, managed parkland and a nature reserve.

Hampton's hive of activity

> *Firemen who had battled for hours to bring a fire under control in Hampton-in-Arden . . . were finally beaten back – by a swarm of wasps.*
>
> *Several officers were badly stung after they disturbed the wasps'nest while trying to secure the roof of one of the three terraced cottages in High Street which had been damaged by the flames.*
>
> *Sub Officer Roger Pratt from Bickenhill station said: "There seemed to be thousands of them. A lot of the lads were stung four or five times, mainly around the neck, and we were forced to give up."*
>
> (News, August 1995)

Jumping the Great Schism

> *Solihull's top clergyman has slammed the Church of England for political correctness – as he confirmed he planned to become a Catholic priest.*
>
> *Canon Peter Hawkins, the 60-year-old married Rector of Solihull – the biggest parish in the Birmingham diocese . . . is resigning in protest at the ordination of women priests.*
>
> *In a statement he said: "We now have a situation in our church where personal rights are allowed to take precedence over divine law."*
>
> (Evening Mail, June 1996)

Big Brother is watching you

> *Home Secretary Michael Howard announced a £160,000 grant to expand Solihull's crime-busting closed circuit television cameras.*
>
> *The Grange will be used to install cameras at five schools, including four on the Tudor Grange campus, three shopping centres and two sports complexes.*
>
> *The borough council also won a separate £23,000 grant to set up cameras in the town centre's civic car park and Station Road shopping parade.*
>
> (Evening Mail, June 1996)

Speed cameras were installed in Coventry Road, Stratford Road and Monkspath Hall road, trapping drivers with photographic evidence.

They had been tried out at the junctions of Kelsey Lane/Kenilworth Road in Balsall Common and Damson Parkway and A45 Coventry Road in 1989 with great success, solving the time-honoured problem of police tackling speeding drivers.

The nineties was the real decade of traffic calming – with humps appearing along suburban routes like Hurdis Road, Burman Road and Bills Lane, Shirley. They were intended to minimise the effect of motorists using them as a "rat run" to avoid the worsening congestion along Stratford Road, where traffic lights often gridlock the town at peak periods, a 30-year-old plan to build a bypass to the west of Shirley being ditched through public opposition.

Beating the burglar

Solihull is set to become the first local authority in Britain to persuade developers to install burglar alarms in all new homes.

New planning chairman Coun Jim Ryan said he wanted Solihull to be first to establish a set of "extras" guidelines for all housebuilders, including smoke alarms.

"I would like to see crime 'designed' out of new estates. It seems crazy to me that developers do not talk to crime prevention officers," he said.

(Evening Mail, May 1996)

Mad cows

A Solihull farmer facing a cash crisis because of the BSE scare is to get his cows to carry advertising hoardings.

Eight of Harry Goode's cattle will be kitted out with special plastic coats bearing advertising logos . . . of Leamington Spa-based marketing consultancy Marketing Net.

The 68-year-old farmer, who has run Box Trees Farm in Stratford Road, Monkspath, for more than 30 years, will then graze the cows in a field alongside the M42 for thousands of passing motorists to see.

(Evening Mail, May 1996)

Brenda's battle

Supermarket giant Asda first angered residents of Haslucks Green Road in the late 1980s, when it made an abortive attempt to build a £5million store on the site of the Territorial Army headquarters in a land-swop deal involving the council.

Householders were again up in arms when Powergen, the privatised successor to the Central Electricity Generating Board, wanted to expand its office block headquarters by the often-badly-congested Stratford Road junction, taking in the closed Reynalds Cross special school site.

The council threw out Powergen's planning application, and the company closed the office and moved out of the borough, jobs and all.

Asda were back in 1995, with plans to demolish the block and school to make way for a hypermarket . . . as neighbours feared that the extra traffic flows would gridlock the area for good despite promises on a new island to replace the existing traffic lights . . .

The president of Shirley Chamber of Trade and by now former mayor three times over Richard Lewis said: "It seems Shirley is becoming a Mecca of supermarkets and these large conglomerates do not take an active part in the community like the small traders, which I think is deplorable."

A heated two-year battle largely fronted by independent councillor Brenda Otton ended with Asda's planning application also being thrown out, and the future of this prime site left uncertain.

A traditional heartland broken

Traditionally, Solihull's affluent southern wards had always been Conservative territory, while the overspill estates of the north returned socialist councillors.

However, inroads into wards like Elmdon, Lyndon and Shirley East were made by opposition parties during the eighties to the point when, after the May 1991 local government elections, the Tories found themselves outnumbered 23–28.

For a year, power was shared between the parties before the Tories regained control courtesy of an alliance with Trevor Eames' Solihull Ratepayers Association group, which had ousted them in Shirley wards.

Coun Brian Chapple became Solihull's first Liberal Democrat mayor after being forced to contest the post with Tory nominee Coun Peter Llewellyn, an unprecedented situation

The local Tory party also split asunder, reflecting the growing national divisions over membership of the European Union. Bob Meacham, who by then had resigned as council leader, quit the party in 1994 and stood as an independent "Stand Up To Brussels" candidate in the European elections.

And then in May 1996 the unthinkable happened.

Local government elections saw the Tories reduced to 16 seats – the same as Labour, with the Liberal Democrats having twelve and the independents six.

Tory leader Ken Meeson lost his seat and the Conservatives found themselves firmly in the minority.

Deflated, they placed themselves into opposition – and history was made when a Labour councillor, Mick Corser, became leader for the first time.

Iain Mills, the popular Tory MP who had represented Meriden constituency since winning it from Labour's John Tomlinson in 1979, was found dead in his London flat on 16 January 1997 after having not been seen by his parliamentary colleagues for three days.

The 56-year-old was found to have drunk more than five times the legal limit for drivers and died of acute alcohol intoxication, an inquest heard.

Local Tories picked bio-technology expert and mother-of-three Caroline Spelman, aged 38, as his successor in the constituency, which readjustments in the eighties had seen it take Knowle, Dorridge and Hockley Heath from its Solihull counterpart . . .

The General Election of 1 May 1997 saw Tony Blair's New Labour romp home to victory with a stunning 178-seat majority, crushing the Tories out of sight in the cities and the Celtic fringe of Scotland, Wales and Cornwall. It was the biggest Labour landslide in the party's history and saw massive swings against the Tories throughout the country as the electorate decided that despite the healthy state of the economy with low inflation, falling inflation and low mortage rates, it was time for a change after 18 years. The imposition of VAT on fuel, disunity in the party's highest ranks over membership of the European Union and a sleaze factor involving several leading Mps had taken their toll.

Yet despite being an outsider from Kent, Mrs Spelman, who had previously contested the unwinnable Labour stronghold of Bassetlaw in Nottinghamshire, defied the trend and held the seat in the face of an 11.57% swing to Labour, whose candidate Brian Seymour-Smith, a Birmingham City Council press officer, lost by just 582 votes after a recount.

Mrs Spelman's achievement made history as she became the first woman MP to represent part of the borough, while the town's MP, John Taylor, was returned with his majority slashed by more than half to a still-comfortable 11,397.

She also became the first MP to speak under new Conservative leader William Hague following his election to replace John Major in June. In her maiden speech Mrs Spelman highlighted the plight of Meriden's green belt as fellow Tories listened to the results of the leadership ballot, and she received a personal thank you from Mr Hague for volunteering to hold the fort while members left the chamber.

She said: 'All too often I am shown new developments where once stood bluebell woods and open fields.'

Beeching Axed

The sweeping rail closures of the 1960s had turned full circle when Chiltern Railways, the privatised successor to British Rail regarding the operation of the Snow Hill-Solihull-London route, announced a new half hourly service from June 1998.

The moves included the relaying of a section of double track near Aylesbury which was scrapped by Dr Beeching and a £250,000 refurbishment of Solihull station itself, described by Solihull and Leamington Rail Users Association chairman Keith Gascoigne as 'a disgrace for many years'.

The new service involved a journey time to one hour 40 minutes from Solihull to Marylebone.

A degree too soon

Nearly 22 years ago Claire Kennedy was Solihull's youngest premature baby ever to survive.

Doctors feared the tiny baby, born three and a half months early and weighing just 1.14lb, would not survive.

But nursing staff at Solihull Hospital battled to keep her alive. And more than two decades later she has proved her fighting spirit by celebrating a 2:1 degree in geography from Birmingham University.

(News, July 1997)

In the heat of the moment

Instead of wedding bells, Solihull bridegroom Adam Smith was greeted by the sound of a fire engine as he waited at the altar of St Alphege's church on Saturday, July 12.

Firemen from Solihull's blue watch came to the rescue after bride-to-be Donna and her father John Elvins were left stranded when their vintage car broke down.

Spotting the chauffeur was missing from the car in New Road, firemen stopped to give the pair a lift.

Surprised bridesmaids watched as bride Donna Smith stepped out of the gleaming machine to tie the knot with her childhood sweetheart.

The bridegroom's brother Lee said: 'It was brilliant. She arrived just in the nick of time. 'We heard the sirens going and the vicar came in and said Donna had just arrived in a fire engine. We thought he was pulling our legs'.

(News, July 1997)

Character building

Bricks from a condemned row of cottages in one of the oldest parts of Solihull town centre have been salvaged in a bid to preserve some of the area's character.

The four cottages in New Road, believed to date back to the early 1800s, were demolished this week after serious subsidence problems were discovered.

The council intended to use the cleared site for an old people's housing development.

But after the personal intervention of planning chairman Coun Jim Ryan (Lab Bickenhill), the cottages' bricks have been carefully saved so they can be used in the replacement building.

The bricks, which the demolition firm was due to sell to a Cornish builder, are now being stored at a council depot.

Coun Ryan said: 'These are lovely handmade bricks and will make the new building on the site more attractive as well as retaining some of the character of old Solihull.

'I would like to see the council do more of this sort of thing in the future.'

(Evening Mail, August 1997)

Illegal or illegitimate?

A Solihull lorry driver who has changed his name by deed poll to Mr Nasty B'stard will be addressed by his new title in court when he appears before magistrates.

B'stard, of Sansome Road, Shirley, who made the switch from Mike Facey to boost his kickboxing career, has denied a charge of driving for too many days without a rest.

His plea was made by post to Wiltshire magistrates court in Chippenham, Wiltshire, and the hearing was adjourned . . .

A court spokesman said that B'stard – who celebrates his 40th birthday on the day of the next hearing – had officially changed his name under the law and would be addressed by the new title in the courtroom.

(Evening Mail, August 1997)

Archer's legacy?

A cut-throat petrol price war in Shirley has claimed the last of the suburb's independently run filling stations.

Rowan Fieldhouse, who had run the Total garage in Stratford Road for more than 20 years, has finally fallen to the rival Sainsbury's and Tesco superstore filling stations.

Mr Fieldhouse had put up a brave four-year fight to stay afloat while watching the suburb's other independent garages go under.

The site of his garage, at the junction with Solihull Road, is now being redeveloped as a Renault car showroom.

(Evening Mail, August 1997)

An apple a day . . .

Supermarket giant Sainsbury is living up to its 'Fresh Ideas' slogan – by submitting plans to build a doctors' surgery in its huge Stratford Road store in Shirley.

If Solihull Council gives the go-ahead it will be the first supermarket surgery of its kind in the Midlands and only the second to be added to an existing UK store.

The surgery would feature state-of-the-art facilities for four local GPs with consulting rooms and a treatment room.

The unusual concept has been drawn up on the back of Government plans to allow GPs to increase the range of services and treatment they offer. Sainsbury has been quick to realise that many GPs, traditionally based in converted houses, do not have the space to expand.

A Sainsbury spokesman said: 'Once it is up and running it will be entirely managed by the health authorities who will pay rent to us. We will simply be the property's landlord.'

Run-of-the-mill customers at the superstore will not be able to seek treatment at the surgery. It will operate along the same lines as existing GP surgeries with customers living in a surrounding catchment area.

(Evening Mail, August 1997)

And for the next century . . .

The relentless attrition between the town and the country which has dominated Solihull for the past century will almost certainly intensify in the next, as the population demands more homes, developers seek bigger profits, the borough council is further pressurised by the Government to release more land for building and environmental groups like the Green Belt Defenders get even sharper.

Many people living in the rural fringe fear that the urban area may be allowed to expand south to the M42 which may become a convenient barrier to further growth. It is somewhat disturbing to look back and that modern suburbs like Olton, Yardley and Acocks Green were villages in the years covered by the first chapter of this book.

Theirs could be the fate of Lapworth, Hockley Heath, and Tanworth-in-Arden in the coming decades if a permanent compromise is not found. Reycling of land throughout the existing urban area rather than allowing developers the easy option of building on farmland surely must be prioritised.

Solihull Council has relentlessly strived to preserve the green belt Meriden Gap dividing its part of the Birmingham conurbation from Coventry, yet new development has been allowed to spill over into Hockley Heath parish, where residents value their green acres just as much as their counterparts to the east.

And just as Birmingham has been the perennial bogey man in the background ready to ride roughshod over its southern neighbour to accommodate its expansion plans on so many occasions, Solihull itself could well become the feared empire builder eyeing up the territory of others.

Solihull has risen to prominence in recent years because of its excellent communications – an airport, three railway lines and its unrivalled position at the hub of the nation's motorway network. It also offers a superb quality of life through its unique blend of urbs in rure.

The borough must never denigrate that quality by allowing that delicate balance to tip in the wrong direction.

FACES

Thomas Beedle Harvey Brooks (Chapter 1/2)
Rev Charles Octavius Richard Wormald in First World War uniform. He married Rev Harvey Brooks'
daughter Ada in 1910. (Chapter 2/3)
Adrian Ellison, Solihull's Olympic goldwinning cox (Chapter 9)
Vikki Chambers who played Sally Waterman in Coronation Street. (Chapter 9)
Shirley girl Mandy Rice-Davies. (Chapter 7).
Caroline Spelman, Solihull's first woman MP elected 1 May 1997.

Robin Jones

True Blue Solihull as seen by the Red Army

Following the overthrow of communism by Boris Yeltsin in 1991 and the subsequent break-up of the Soviet Union, many artefacts of the old regime found their way out of secret files in exchange for western currency.

Among them was a series of scale maps produced for the Red Army on the lines of our own Ordnance Survey. Unlike the Ordnance Survey, the Soviet maps included military installations and other features like armament factories wherever appropriate.

This extract from a 1:25,000 map of the West Midlands highlights factories like the giant Land Rover plant in Lode Lane, the Highlands Road industrial estate in Shirley and the nearby Lucas Research establishment in Dog Kennel Lane – sites that might well have been given somewhat closer attention in the event of hostilities breaking out.

The meticulous mapmakers of the Cold War era have, however, missed other local places of military interest, such as the Royal Observer Corps underground monitoring bunker in the fields between Dog Kennel Lane and Cheswick Green, where volunteers would have measured the effects of a nuclear strike on Birmingham, and the ugly concrete government supplies depot in Stratford Road, Shirley, alongside Shirley Heath junior school (picture above).

That building baffled local residents when it was erected in the early fifties without official explanation. It is now used as a depot for the gas pipeline company Transco.

Although dated 1977, the Red Army map appears to be loosely based on the Ordnance Survey 1:25,000 map of 1951, (reprinted 1960 with minor corrections), although several later features have been added.

Take Shirley's Cranmore estate for instance. The Soviet map shows Twinderrow's pool which had long since been filled in by 1977, and also the Cran Brook running through the Swallows Meadow housing estate, even though it had bee culverted there 25 years before. Yet later minor additions such as Brownley Road cul-de-sac, and the Witehouse Way estate off Blossomfield Road, Solihull, are pinpointed with accuracy. Very strange.

Also, the layout of Cheswick Green is only a crude approximation of the old Mount estate, which had largely vanished by the early seventies. Yet the Tudor Grange running track, not on the 1:25,000 OS map available at the time, is featured.

The Russian text describes Solihull as having a population of 110,400 – data compiled before it became a metropolitan borough in 1974. It also makes much of the fact that houses in the Birmingham conurbation had piped water, electricity, gas and telephone connections – something that the great 'superpower' obviously thought to be remarkable for ordinary people.

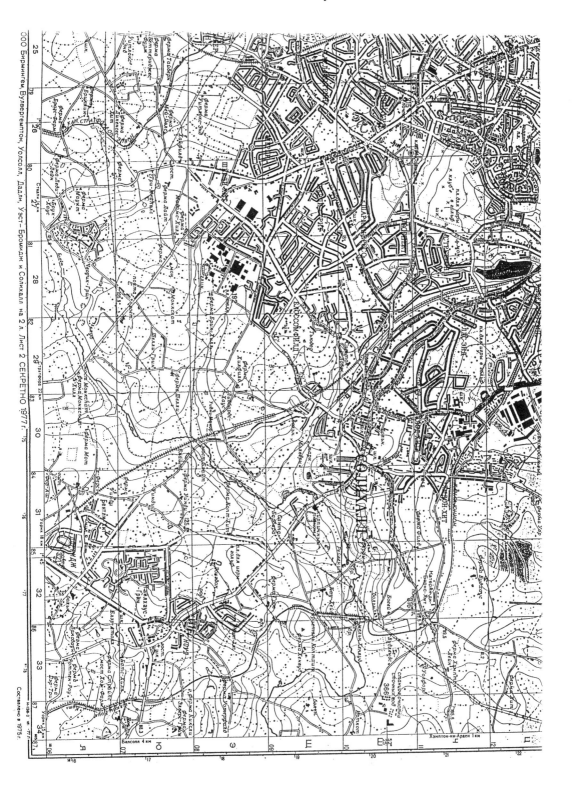

REMEMBER ME THIS WAY...

The world was left numb on the morning of 31 August 1997 by the scarcely believable news that Diana, Princess of Wales, had died following a high-speed car accident in Paris. As shock and bewilderment gave way to anger, nations right across the globe were united in mourning the loss of a woman who had seized their imagination and touched their hearts on so many occasions.

In Solihull, as elsewhere, residents flocked to express their sorrow and dismay at such a devastating and utterly purposeless loss of life.

The acres of flower bouquets that adorned green spaces in front of London's royal palaces were mirrored in Solihull town centre, where the War Memorial became a mountain of floral tributes. Flowers, wreaths and messages of sympathy piled up beside the cross on Meriden's famous green, in Chelmsley Wood shopping centre and also in Mell Square. Condolence books were opened at St Alphege church and borough libraries to be sent to Buckingham Palace, flags flew at half mast and a minute's silence was observed at the start of the borough council meeting on the following Tuesday.

Saturday 5 September left Solihull a ghost town, as council buildings apart from the Register Office remained closed as a mark of respect, sports fixtures and fetes were postponed and many shops and stores closed their doors until 2pm if not all day during an unprecedented public outpouring of grief on the day of the funeral.

The Mayor of Solihull, Councillor Peter Hogarth, attended a requiem eucharist at St Alphege church on the morning.

Rector Tony Wilds said: 'She cared about what we should be concerned about, such as the unfortunate, poor and other victims.'

During one of her visits to the borough, on 31 July 1992, Diana had opened the Wooden Spoon Centre, an educational unit for special needs children in Lode Lane. Centre head Sue Maiden said: 'She was absolutely superb with the children and took time to speak to every child present – there must have been about 60 there.'

A previous visit, on 8 March 1990, saw Diana greeted by flag-waving crowds when she visited the Juvenile Centre in Chelmsley Wood. Shown round by principal officer Steve Hodges, Diana spent more than an hour talking to youngsters there, many of who had suffered abuse at home, problems at school, or who had been in trouble with the police and were on a supervision programme.

At the door, she was presented with a bouquet of flowers by three-year-olds Ricky Wiggell and Katy Berry, who, as the picture shows, became somewhat overawed by the occasion.

Happy scenes like these will be the way in which Solihull people will surely remember the People's Princess.